RECORD OFFICES:

HOW TO FIND THEM

THIRD EDITION

Jeremy Gibson

and

Pamela Peskett

Federation of
Family History Societies
1985

Published by the

Federation of Family History Societies,
96 Beaumont Street, Milehouse, Plymouth PL2 3AQ, England

First edition, 1981
Second edition, 1982, reprinted 1983
Third edition, 1985

ISBN 0 907099 40 8

Maps devised and drawn by Pamela Peskett

Typing and layout by Jeremy Gibson

Printed by Parchment (Oxford) Limited

Acknowledgments

Our gratitude goes first to all those archivists who kindly supplied maps issued by their individual offices or specially prepared for us; and who subsequently checked our redrawn versions, correcting and up-dating these. We are grateful too to Duncan Harrington for help with the map of Canterbury; and to our archivist (who remains anonymous by his own request) for his advice (page 4) on how to behave in a record office.

This third edition has revised maps of central London (showing the new location of the Society of Genealogists), Worcester (showing the new County Record Office), and Edinburgh; and additional maps of Barrow-in-Furness and Grimsby. Once again we would like to thank our families, Miss Helen Gibson, for further help with lettering of the names of towns, and Hugh Peskett, for help with the map of Edinburgh.

Contents

Some Do's and Don'ts of using Record Offices and Archives Departments

To some family historians, using record offices is a new experience and one for which many are unprepared. Offices all have their particular rules and regulations which you should find out about and observe, but here are some of the more generally accepted guidelines which genealogists need to follow:

1. Go armed with several pencils (use of pens generally forbidden) and plenty of paper. Some archivists do not have supplies of these to lend to searchers.
2. Have a hearty breakfast and take a packed lunch (no food or drink to be consumed while working with records) - your time will be limited, so make the most of it.
3. Go with a list of objectives; make them as brief as possible. Don't spend time relating the whole history of your family to the archivist. He will respond more readily to specific questions regarding sources for a particular problem you have.
4. Don't expect to have a mountain of records to plough through at the drop of a hat. Many offices limit the number of records you may use at any one time. Be patient - records will be produced as quickly as the staff's time permits. Plan ahead - use the time in between for browsing in the office library among secondary sources - directories, local histories and indexes.
5. Treat all records with respect; sometimes it will not be possible to see the originals because of their fragile condition. The archivist may insist that you use transcripts or microfilms; if you need to clarify a point, ask to see the original for a specific reason.
6. Take along plenty of cash; photocopies and certificates are not cheap, and if you need to purchase them, the archivist will need to have his cash before he hands them over.
7. Above all, do not assume that the record office you wish to visit will be open on the day you have planned to visit it. Ring the office first and make an appointment (even though this is not always necessary); check on the opening hours and lunchtime closures (many have restricted hours because of financial cutbacks). Check whether you need to book a microfilm reader when registers are only available on microfilm.

Remember, archivists are only human and not record-producing automatons; treat them with respect and you will get service accordingly.

Avon

Bristol Record Office, The Council House, College Green, Bristol BS1 5TR (0272 26031 ext 442)

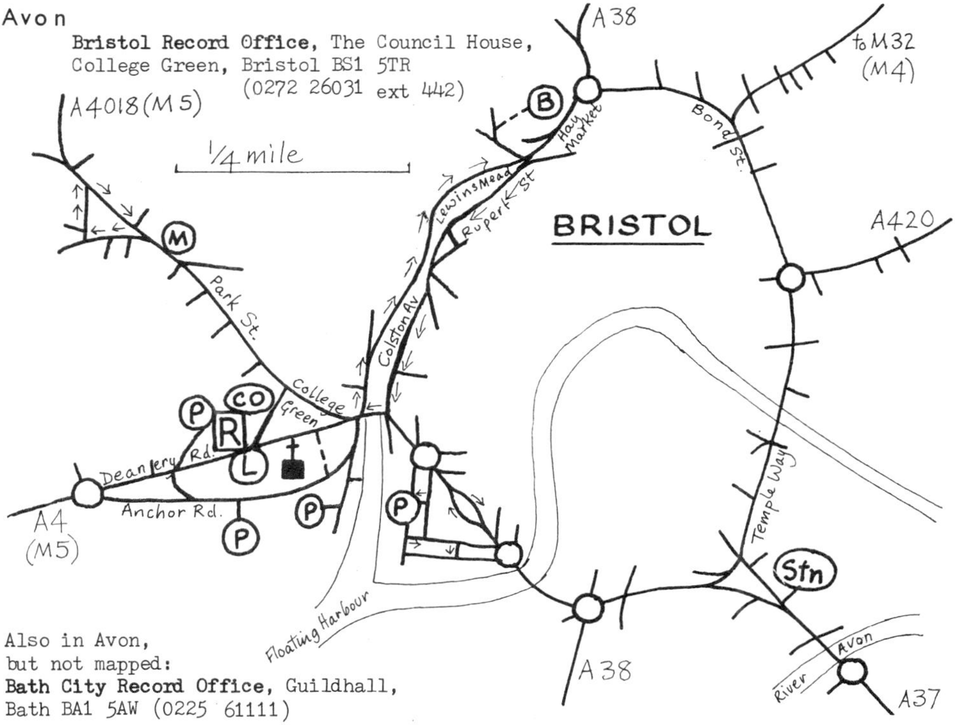

Also in Avon, but not mapped:
Bath City Record Office, Guildhall, Bath BA1 5AW (0225 61111)

Bedfordshire

Bedfordshire Record Office, County Hall, Bedford MK42 9AP (0234 63222 ext 277)

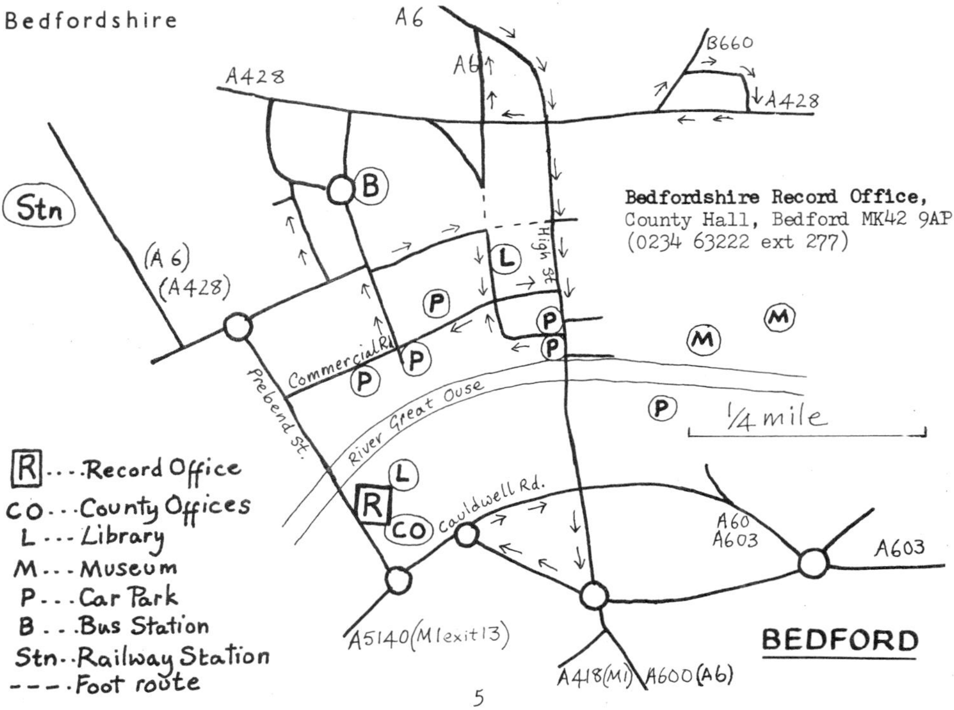

Berkshire

Berkshire Record Office,
Shire Hall, Shinfield Park,
Reading RG2 9XD
(0734 875444 ext 3182)

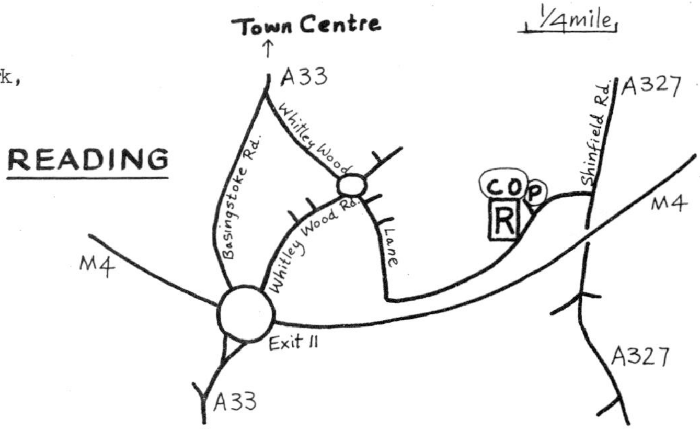

R ... Record Office
CO ... County Offices
L ... Library
M ... Museum
P ... Car Park
B ... Bus Station
Stn .. Railway Station
---- Foot route

"Sources for Genealogy in the Berkshire Record Office", 1979, 60p + postage.
"Parish Registers of the Archdeaconry of Berkshire: A handlist", 1981, 40p + postage.

Buckinghamshire

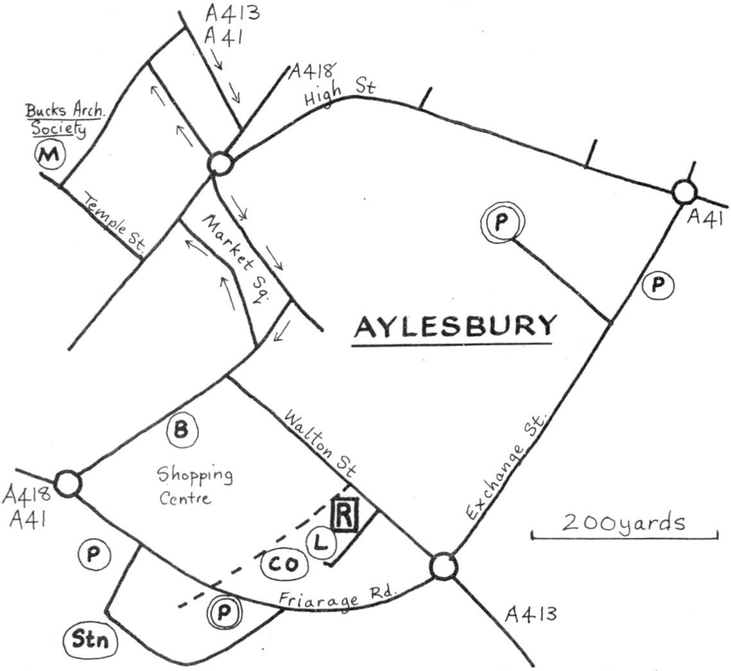

Buckinghamshire Record Office,
County Hall, Aylesbury HP20 1UA
(0296 5000 ext 586)

"Notes for the Guidance of Genealogists"

Buckinghamshire Archaeological Society,
The Museum, Church Street,
Aylesbury

Cambridgeshire

"Genealogical Sources in Cambridgeshire", Michael Farrar, Cambs. R.O., 1979, (out of print).

Cambridge County Record Office,
Shire Hall,
Castle Hill,
Cambridge CB3 0AP
(0223 317281)

Cambridge University Library,
West Road,
Cambridge CB3 9DR
(0223 61441)
(Ely diocesan records)
(reader's ticket necessary)

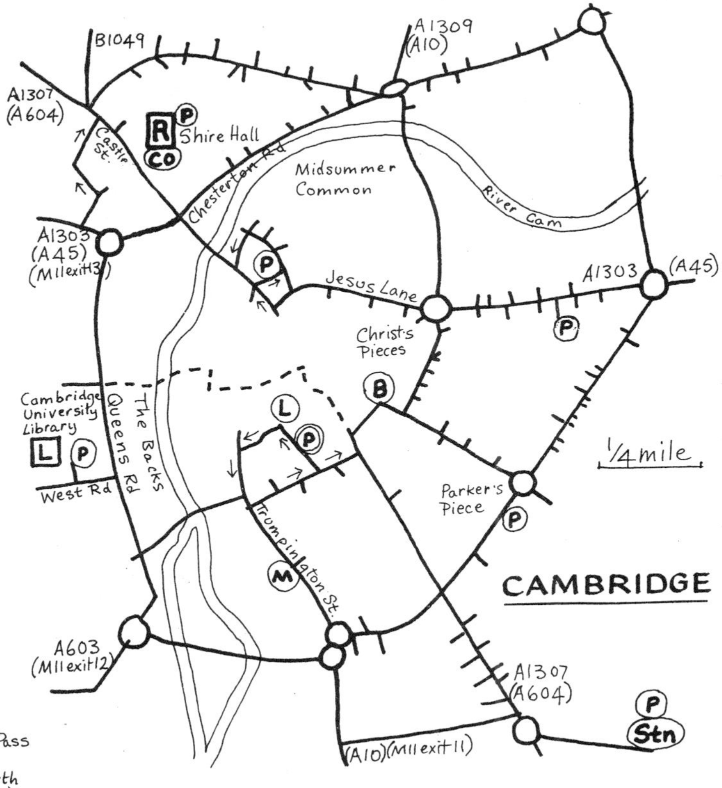

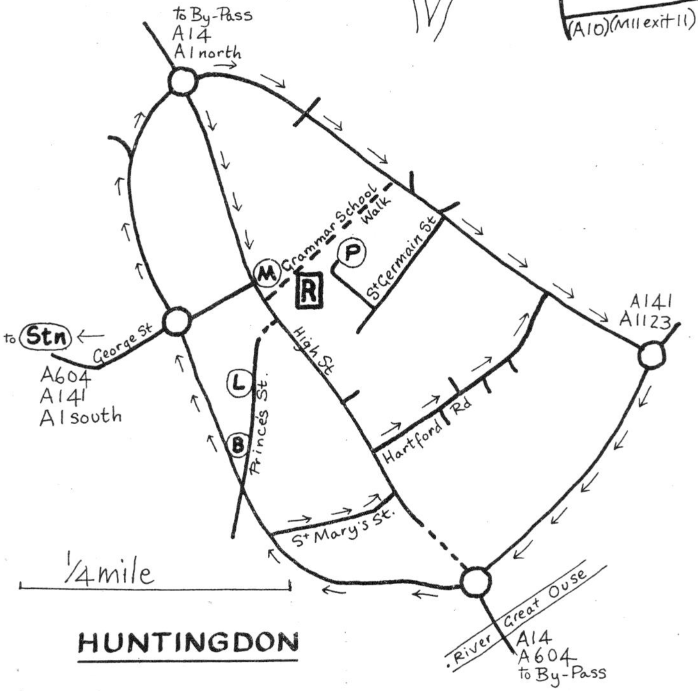

Cambridge County Record Office (Huntingdon branch)
Grammar School Walk
Huntingdon PE18 6LF
(0480 52181)

Cheshire

Cheshire Record Office,
The Castle,
Chester CH1 2DN
(0244 602574)

Sources sheets on records

Chester City Record Office,
Town Hall,
Chester CH1 2HJ
(0244 40144)

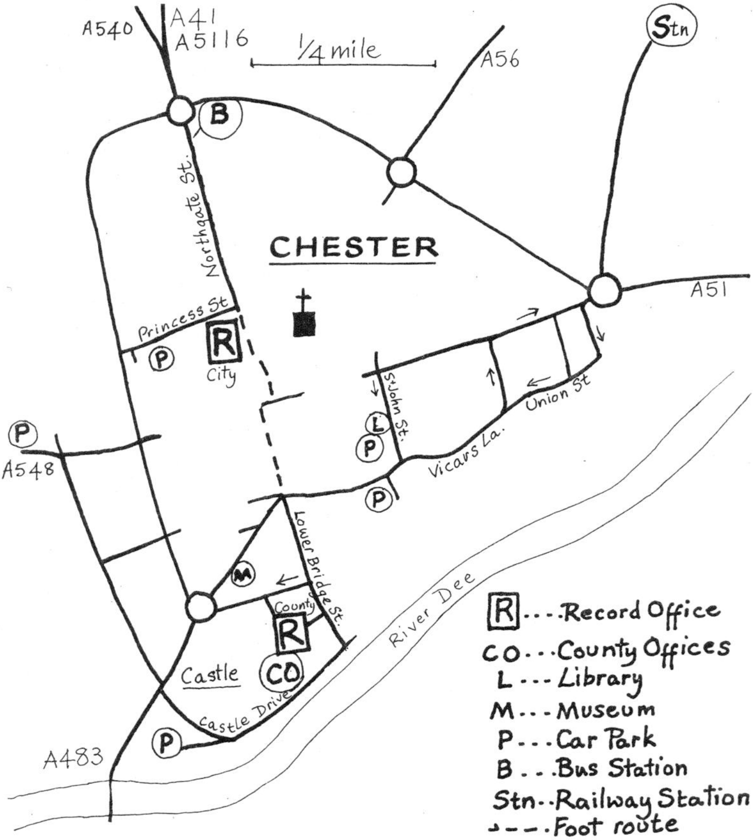

Cleveland

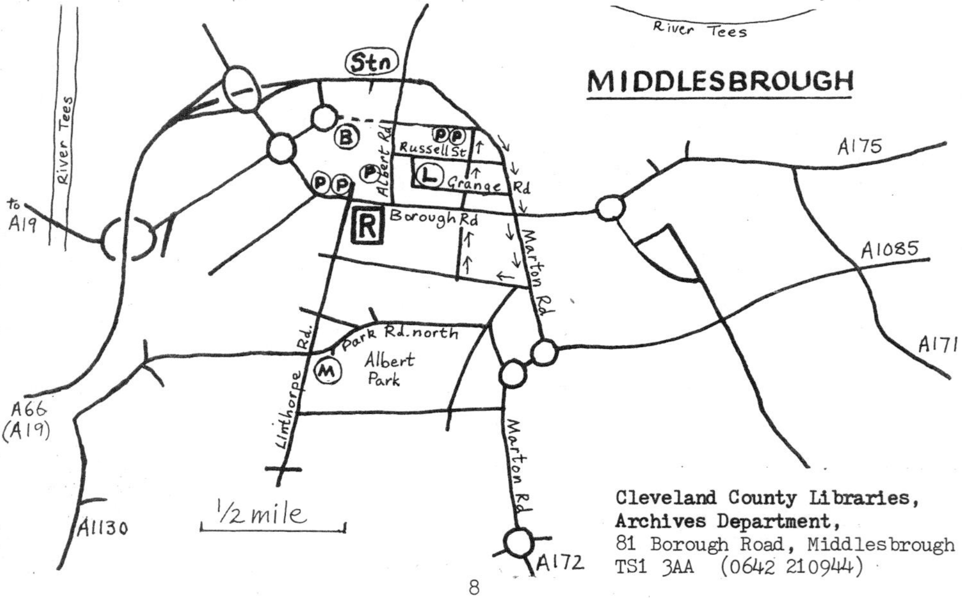

Cleveland County Libraries, Archives Department,
81 Borough Road, Middlesbrough
TS1 3AA (0642 210944)

Cornwall

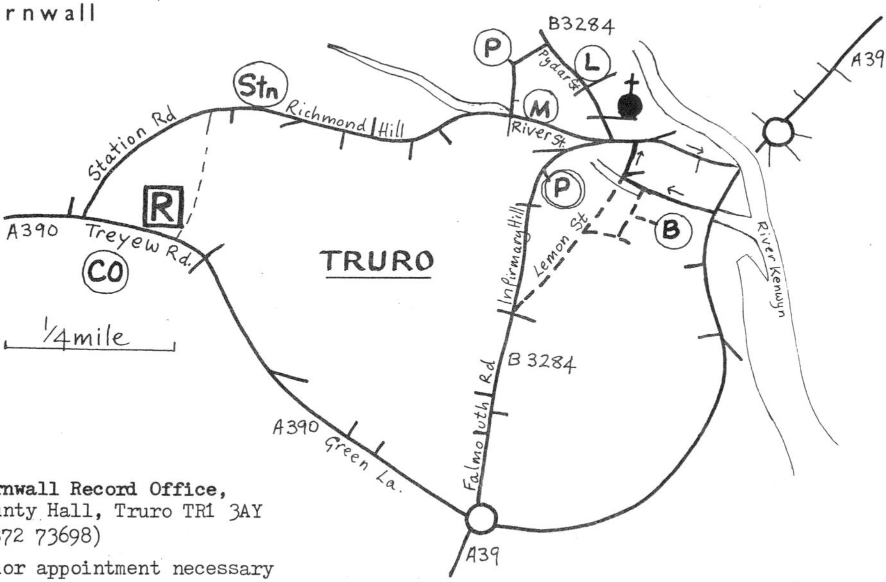

Cornwall Record Office,
County Hall, Truro TR1 3AY
(0872 73698)
Prior appointment necessary

Cumbria

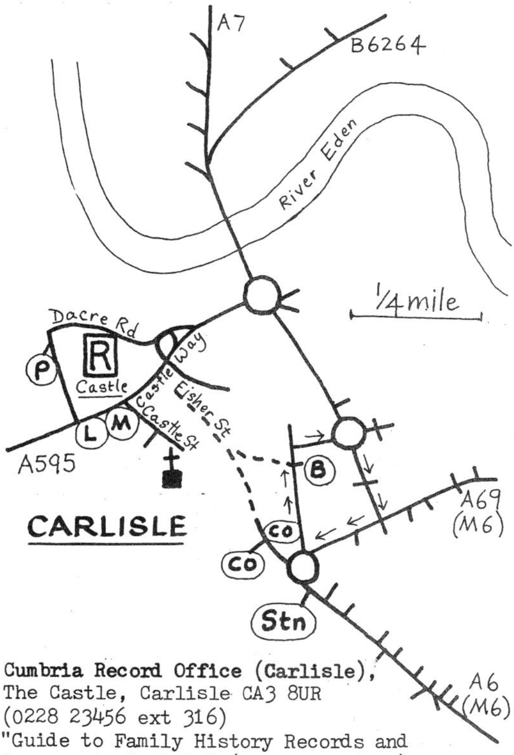

Cumbria Record Office (Carlisle),
The Castle, Carlisle CA3 8UR
(0228 23456 ext 316)
"Guide to Family History Records and Sources in Cumbria" (in preparation)

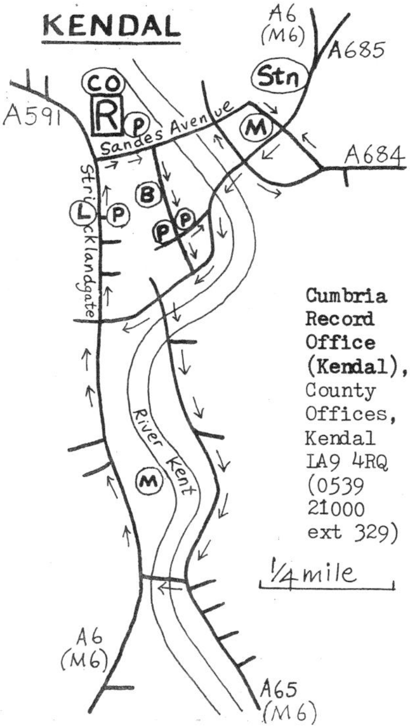

Cumbria Record Office (Kendal),
County Offices,
Kendal
LA9 4RQ
(0539
21000
ext 329)

Cumbria

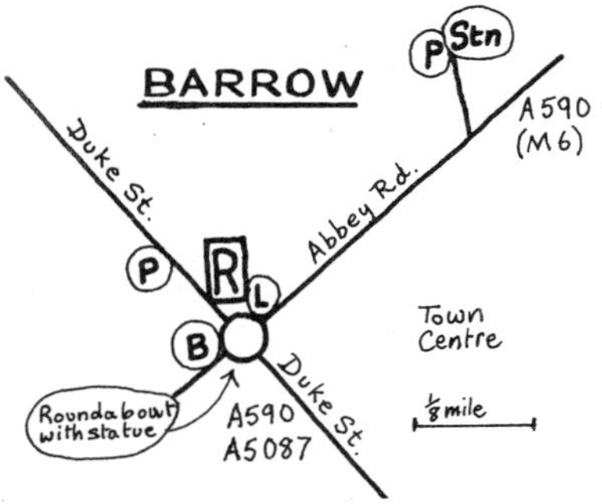

Cumbria Record Office
(Barrow branch),
140 Duke Street,
Barrow in Furness
LA14 1XW
(0229 31269)

Derbyshire

Derbyshire Record Office,
County Offices,
Matlock DE4 3AG
(0629 3411 ext 7347)
(entrance on Smedley Street)

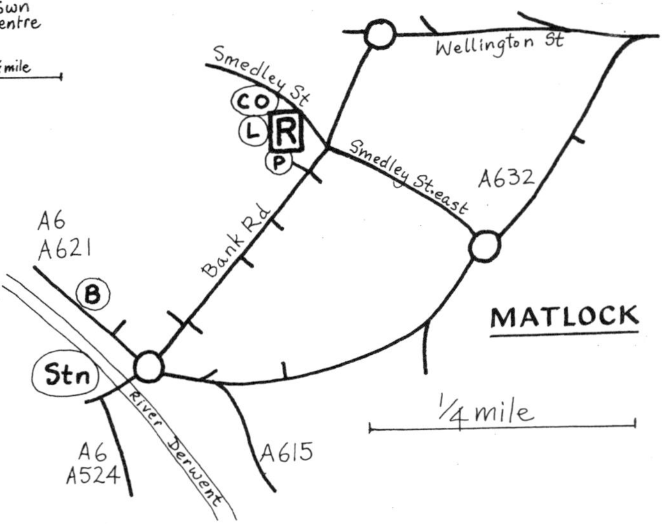

Dorset

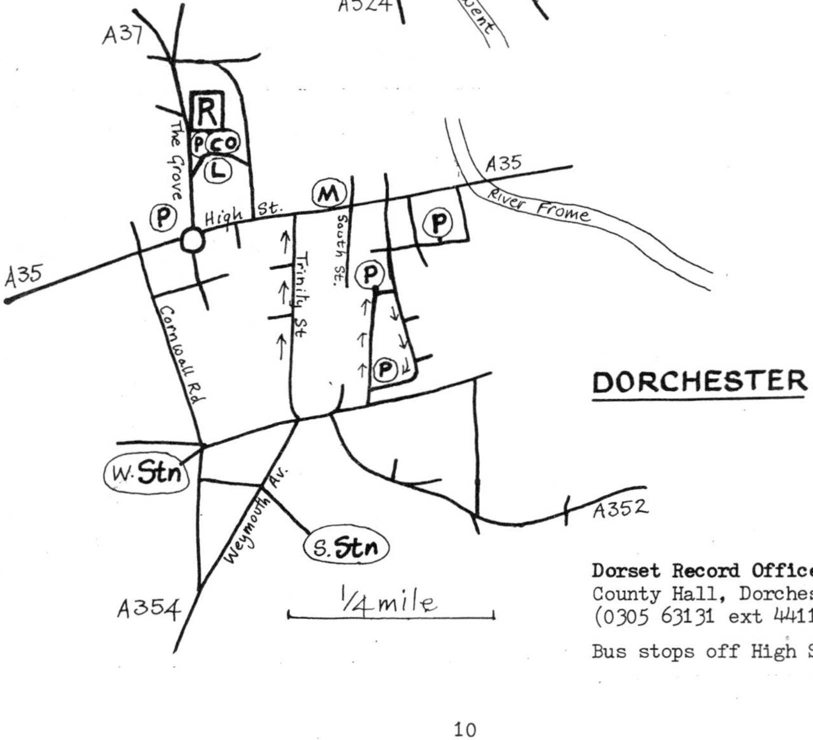

Dorset Record Office,
County Hall, Dorchester DT1 1XJ
(0305 63131 ext 4411)

Bus stops off High Street

Devon

Devon Record Office, Castle Street, Exeter EX4 3PQ
(0392 53509) Some documents require 24 hours notice.

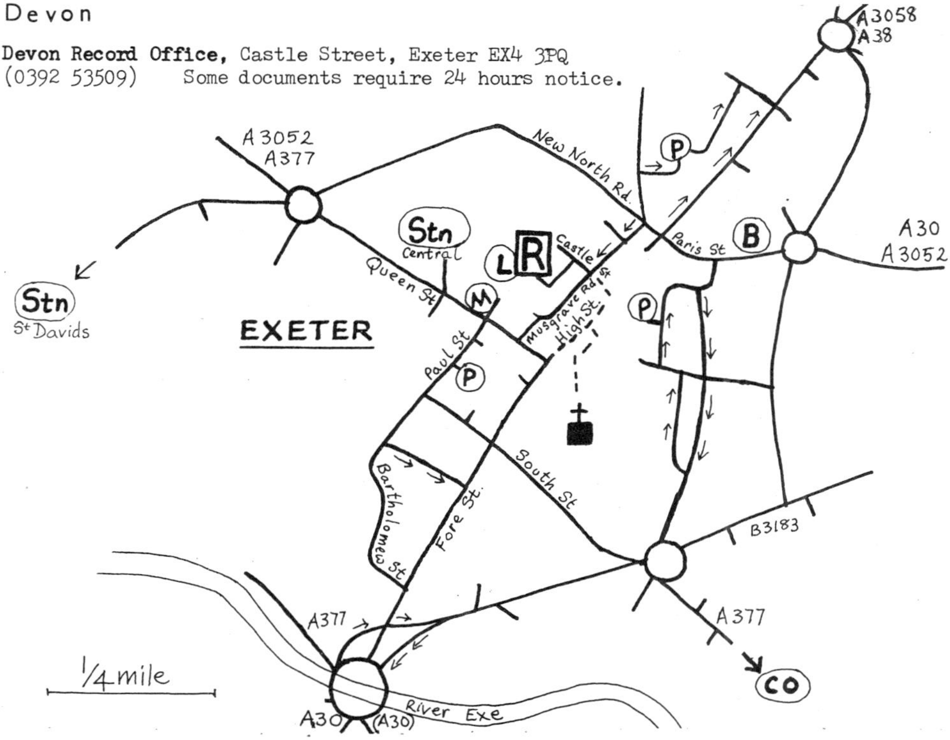

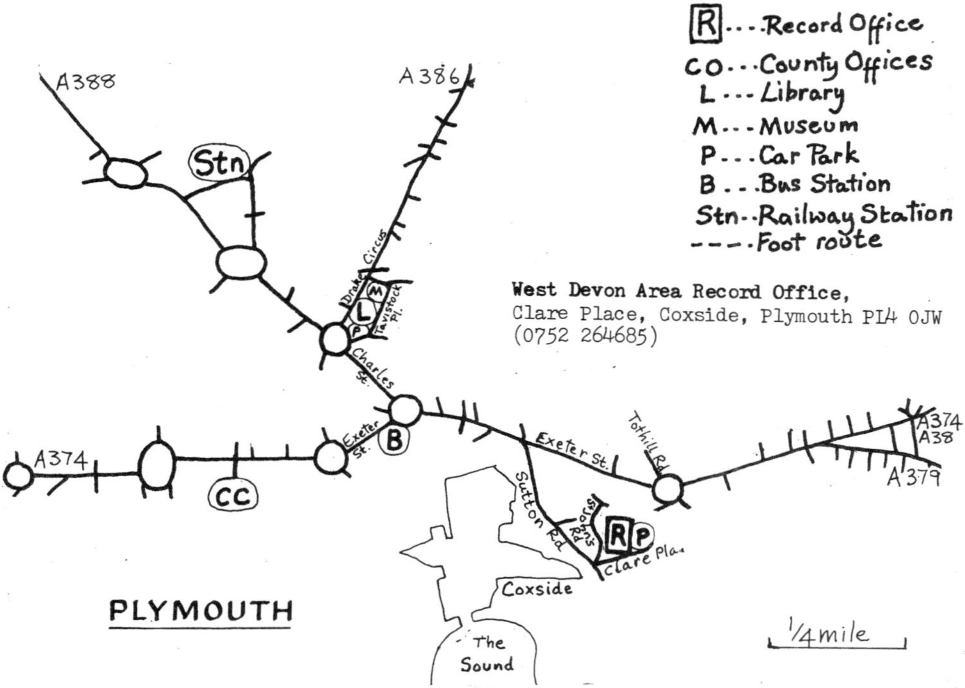

West Devon Area Record Office,
Clare Place, Coxside, Plymouth PL4 0JW
(0752 264685)

Co. Durham

Durham County Record Office, County Hall,
Durham DH1 5UL
(0385 64411)

DP = University of Durham Department of Palaeography and Diplomatic, housed in two buildings:
The Prior's Kitchen,
The College,
Durham DH1 3EQ
(0385 64561); and
5 The College,
Durham DH1 3EQ
(0385 61478). These are in the Cathedral precincts: 5 The College is on the left of the quadrangle; The Prior's Kitchen is off the South Cloister.

Parking is not allowed in the College.

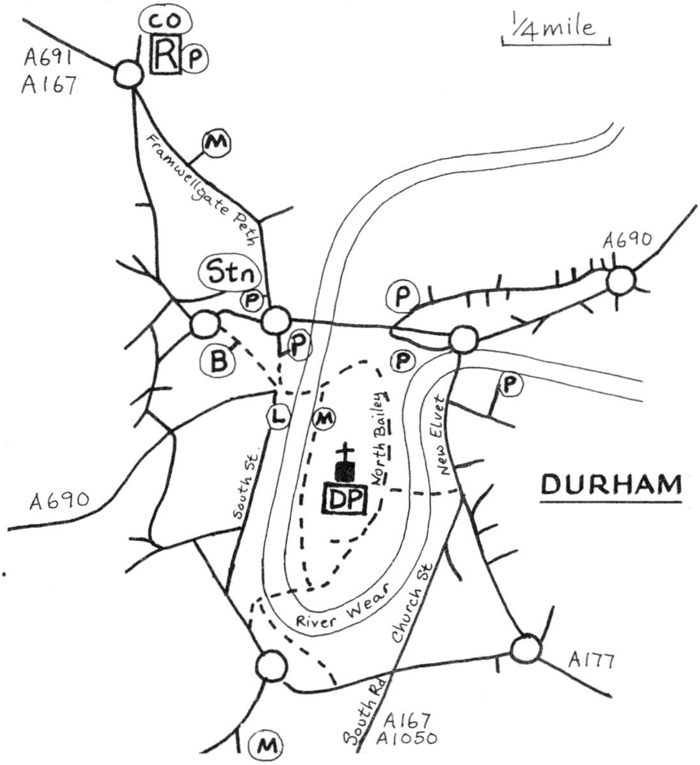

Essex

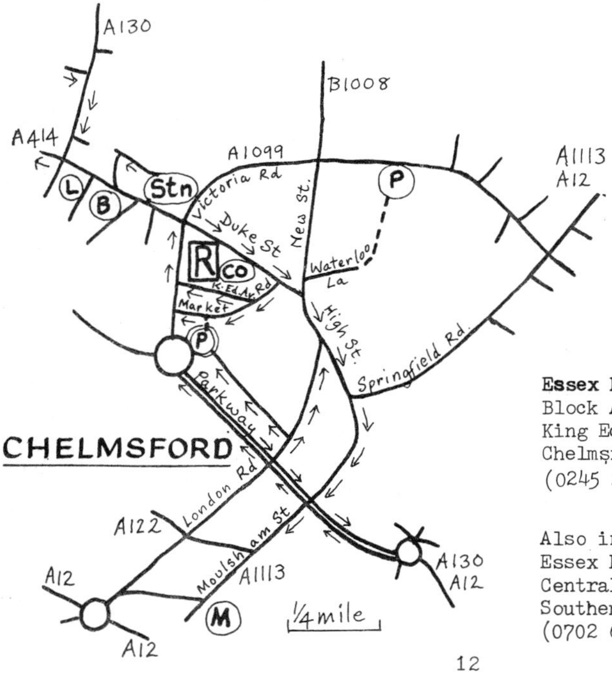

- R ... Record Office
- CO ... County Offices
- L ... Library
- M ... Museum
- P ... Car Park
- B ... Bus Station
- Stn .. Railway Station
- ---- Foot route

Essex Record Office,
Block A, County Hall,
King Edward Avenue,
Chelmsford CM1 1LX
(0245 267222 ext 2104)

Also in Essex, but not mapped:
Essex Record Office, Southend Branch
Central Library, Victoria Avenue,
Southend-on-Sea, Essex SS2 6EX
(0702 612621 ext 49)

Gloucestershire

Gloucestershire Record Office, Kingsholm, Worcester Street, Gloucester GL1 3DW (0452 21444)

"Gloucestershire Family History", 1979, £1.50 + 20p post (110g).

Parking at the Record Office, enter from Alvin Street.
Access by footpath only from Worcester Street.

Modern records are at the Shire Hall (CO) for which an appointment must be made.

The City Library (L) administers the large local history 'Gloucestershire Collection'.

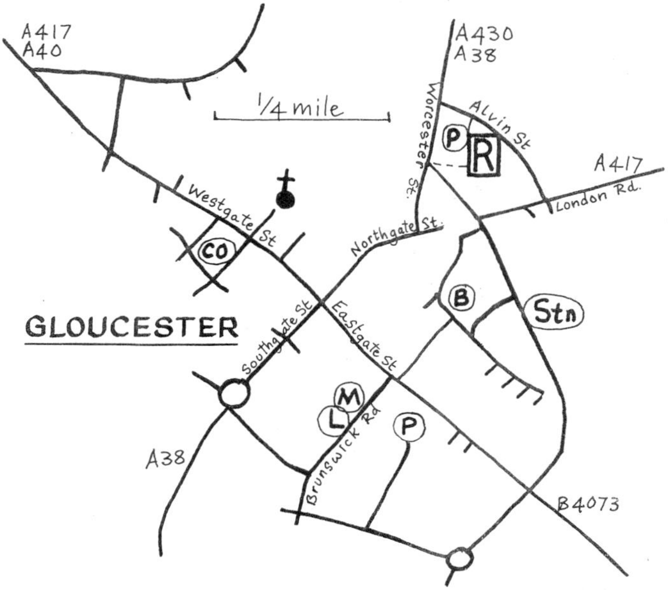

Hampshire

Hampshire Record Office, 20 Southgate Street (formerly St Thomas' Church), Winchester SO23 9EF (0962 63153)

"Sources for Genealogy"

See also Portsmouth and Southampton, page 14, and Isle of Wight, page 36.

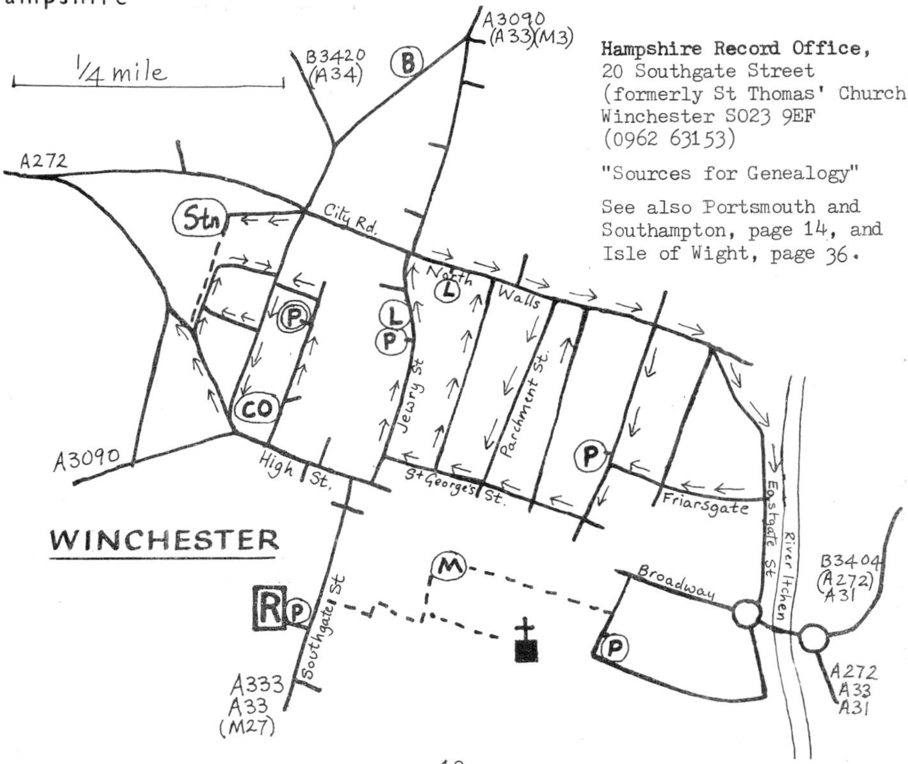

Southampton Civic Record Office,
Civic Centre,
Southampton SO9 4XL
(0703 23855 ext 251)

R . . . Record Office
CO . . . County Offices
L . . . Library
M . . . Museum
P . . . Car Park
B . . . Bus Station
Stn . . Railway Station
- - - . Foot route
C C . . Civic Centre

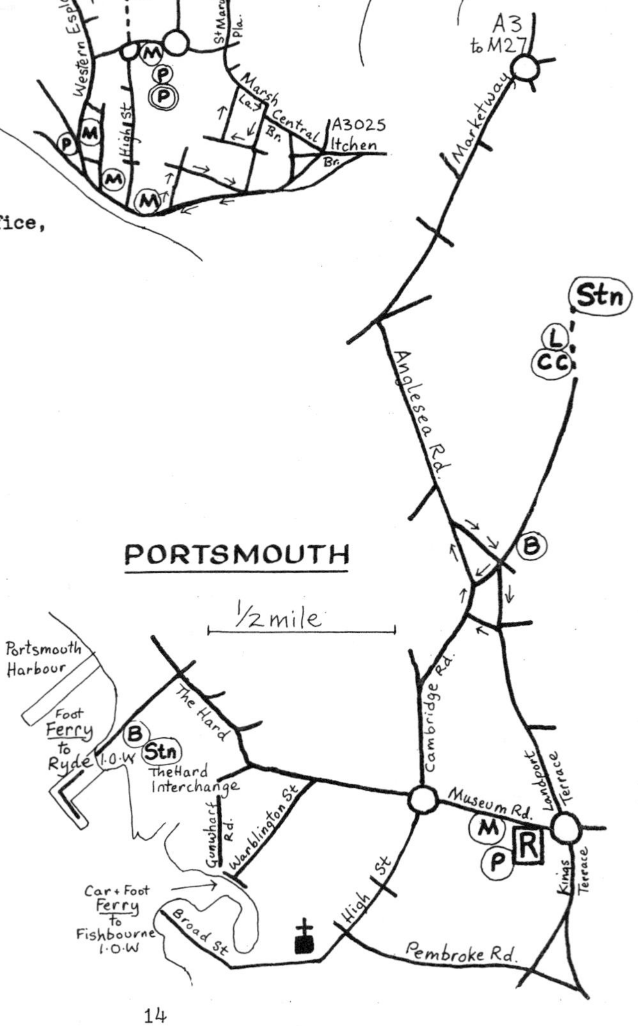

Portsmouth City Records
Office,
3 Museum Road,
Portsmouth PO1 2LE
(0705 829765)

Hereford and Worcester

Hereford and Worcester Record Office (Hereford branch),
The Old Barracks,
Harold Street,
Hereford HR1 2QX
(0432 265441)

Car parking at the Record Office

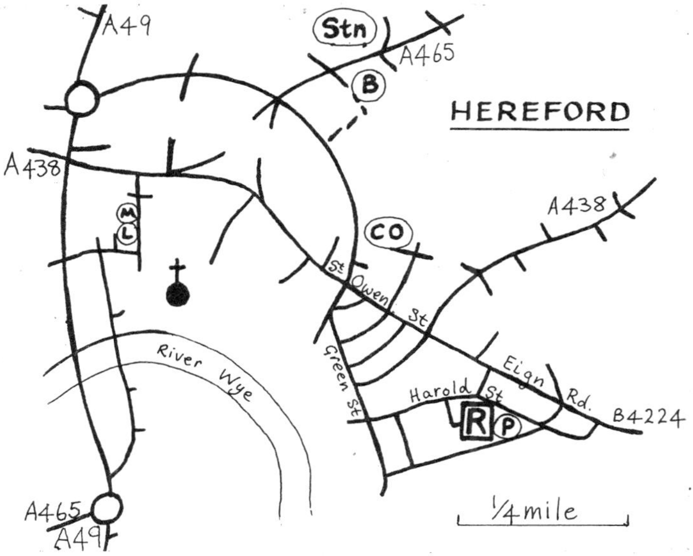

County of Hereford and Worcester Record Office:

Worcester Headquarters, County Hall, Spetchley Road, Worcester WR5 2NP (0905 353366 ext 3612)

Holdings include Quarter Sessions records and original parish registers. Also microfilm of parish registers, bishop's transcripts, census returns, and newspapers. IGI microfiche for UK.

Worcester Branch, St Helen's, Fish Street, Worcester WR1 2HN (0905 353366 ext 3616)

St Helen's is a converted church in a pedestrian area just off the main shopping street. Limited car parking nearby.

Holdings include diocesan records (bishop's transcripts, probate and tithe records); nonconformist records; Worcester city archives. Also microfilm of parish registers, census returns; microfiche of IGI for UK.

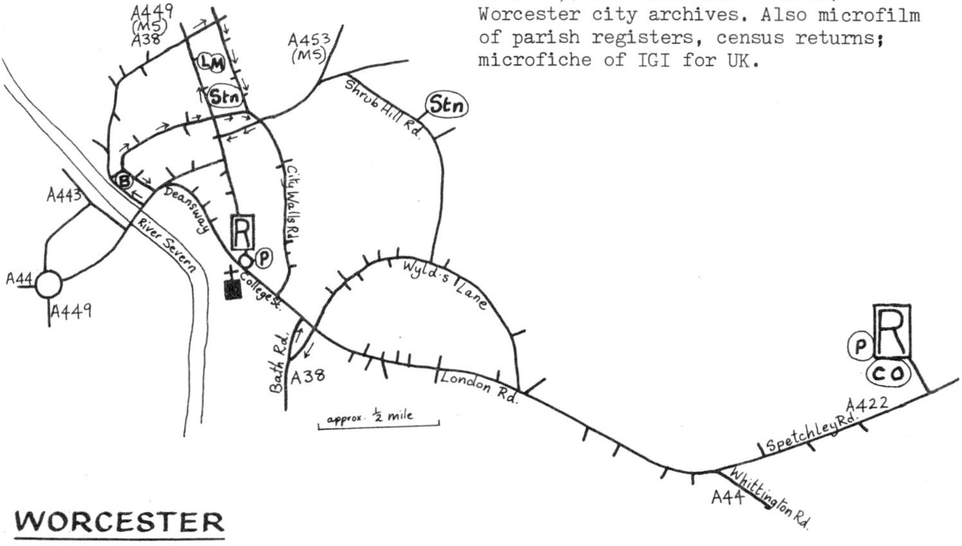

Hertfordshire

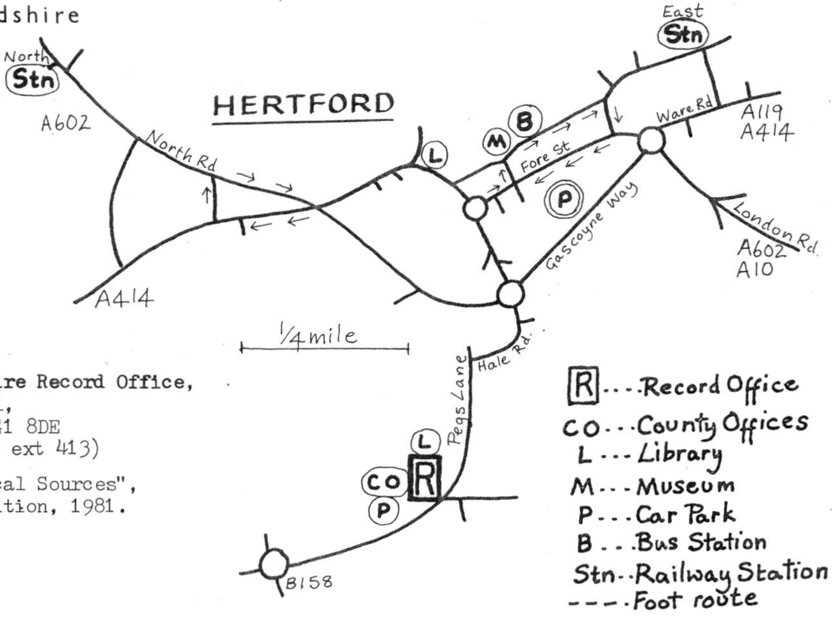

Hertfordshire Record Office,
County Hall,
Hertford SG1 8DE
(0992 54242 ext 413)

"Genealogical Sources",
Revised edition, 1981.

Humberside

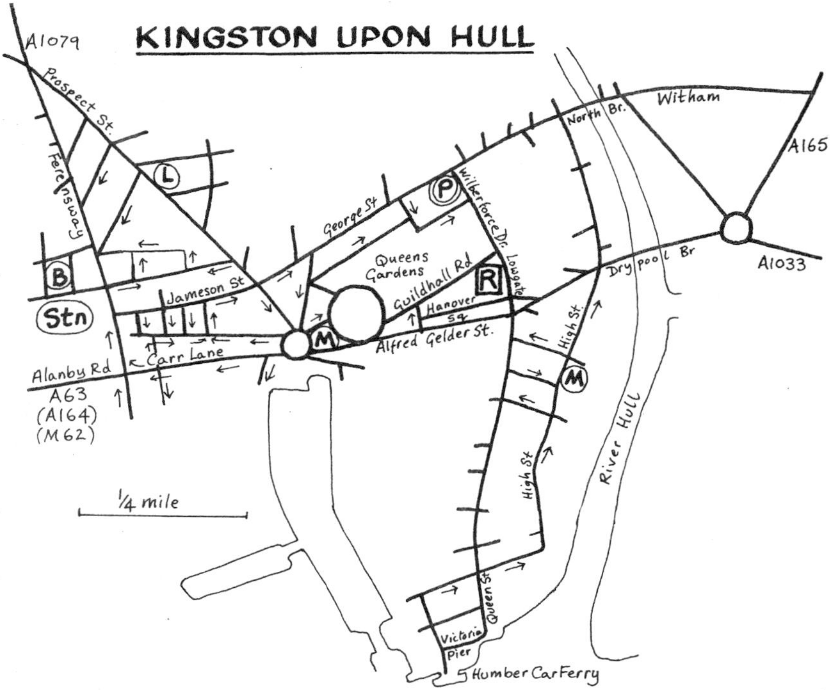

Kingston upon Hull City Record Office,
79 Lowgate, Kingston upon Hull HU1 2AA
(0482 222015)

Humberside

Humberside County Record Office,
County Hall, Beverley HU17 9BA
(0482 867131 ext 3393/4)

Below:

South Humberside Area Record Office,
Town Hall Square,
Grimsby DN31 1HX
(0472 53481)

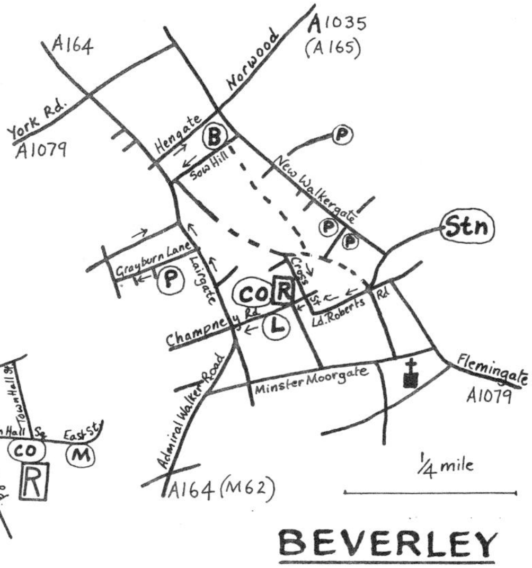

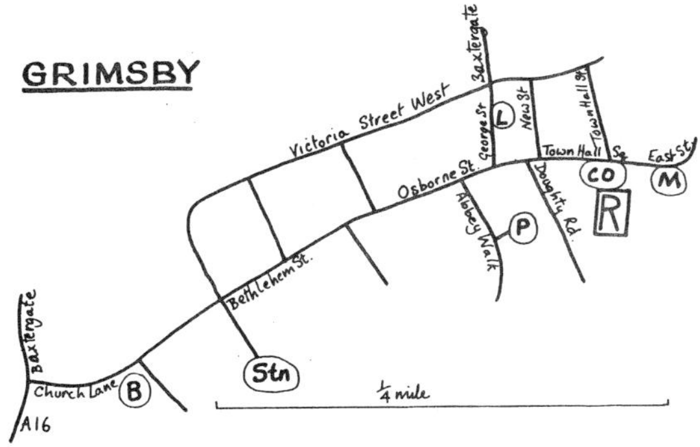

Kent

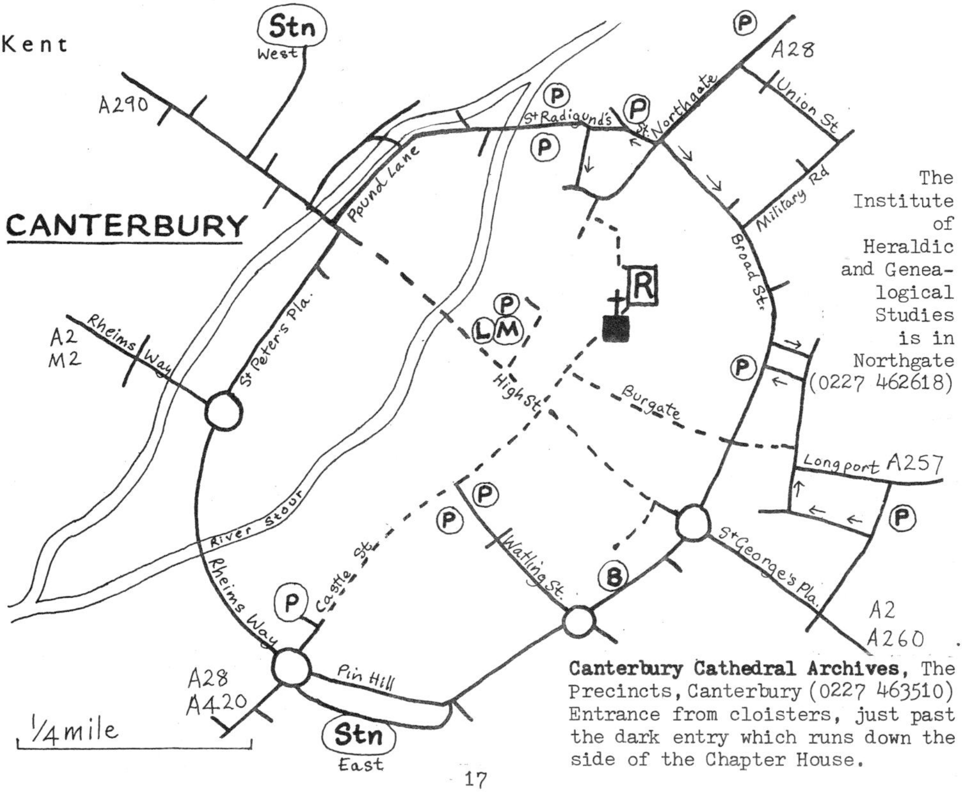

The Institute of Heraldic and Genealogical Studies is in Northgate (0227 462618)

Canterbury Cathedral Archives, The Precincts, Canterbury (0227 463510) Entrance from cloisters, just past the dark entry which runs down the side of the Chapter House.

Kent

Kent County Archives Office, County Hall,
Maidstone ME14 1XH
(0622 671411)

Traffic can be very congested, so visitors approaching from the opposite side of the town are advised to park on that side and walk through the town centre.

Also in Kent, unmapped:
Branches of Kent Archives Office
at Folkestone and Ramsgate Libraries

Lancashire

Lancashire Record Office,
Bow Lane, Preston PR1 8ND
(0772 54868)

"Handlist of Genealogical Sources"

Leicestershire

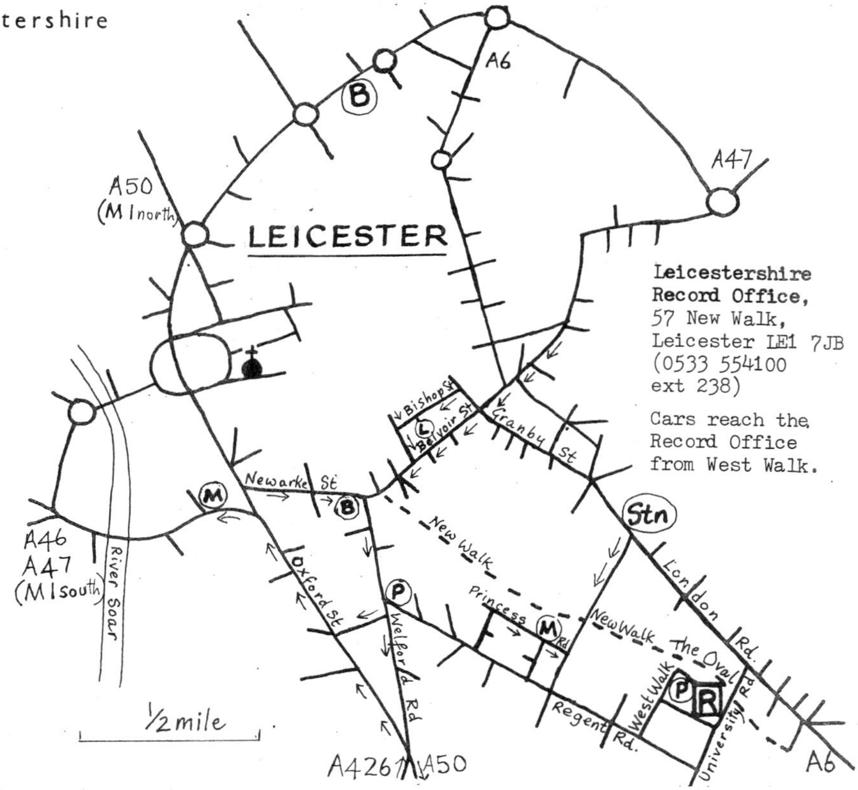

Leicestershire Record Office,
57 New Walk,
Leicester LE1 7JB
(0533 554100
ext 238)

Cars reach the Record Office from West Walk.

Lincolnshire

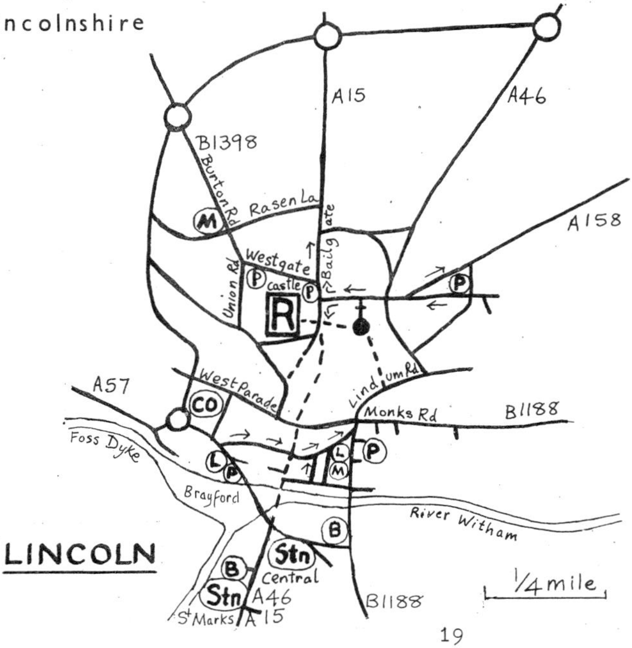

R ... Record Office
CO ... County Offices
L ... Library
M ... Museum
P ... Car Park
B ... Bus Station
Stn .. Railway Station
- - - - Foot route

Lincolnshire Archives Office, The Castle,
Lincoln LN1 3AB
(0522 25158)

The Archives Office is in the red brick building on your left as you enter the Castle Grounds.

"Your Family History in Lincolnshire Archives"

Key

6 **British Library, Department of Manuscripts,**
Great Russell Street, WC1B 3DG (01-636 1544)
14 **College of Arms,** Queen Victoria Street, EC4V 4BT (01-248 2762)
8 **Corporation of London Records Office,** P.O. Box 270, Guildhall, EC2P 2EJ (01-606 3030 ext 2251)(in Room 221, 2nd floor, North Office Block, immediately behind Guildhall, reached from Basinghall Street)
13 **General Register Office** (Office of Population Censuses and Surveys), St Catherine's House, 10 Kingsway, WC2B 6JP (01-242 0262) (for Birth and Marriage Certificates)
12 **G.R.O.,** Alexandra House, Kingsway (for Death Certificates)
3 **Greater London Record Office and History Library,** 40 Northampton Road, EC1 OAB (has its own small car park, free, for use of readers; also NCP nearby)
7 **Guildhall Library,** Aldermanbury, EC2P 2EJ (01-606 3030)
18 **House of Lords Record Office,** SW1A OPW (01-219 3073)
16 **India Office Library and Records,** 197 Blackfriars Road, SW1 8NG (01-928 9531)
20 **Lambeth Palace Library,** SE1 7JU (01-928 6222)
15 **The Principal Registry of the Family Division,** Somerset House, Strand, WC2R 1LP (01-405 7641 ext 3959)
11 **Public Record Office,** Chancery Lane, WC2A 1LR (01-405 0741)
10 **Public Record Office, Census Search Room,** Portugal Street, WC2A (01-405 3488 ext 335)
7 **Royal Commission on Historical Manuscripts** (housing the National Register of Archives, the Manorial Documents Register and the Tithe Documents Register), Quality House, Quality Court, Chancery Lane, EC2A 1HP (01-242 1198)
1 **Society of Friends' Library,** Friends House, Euston Road, NW1 2BJ (01-387 3601)
5 **Society of Genealogists,** 14 Charterhouse Buildings, EC1M 7BA (01-251 8799) (Charterhouse Buildings is a cul-de-sac at the junction of Goswell Road and Clerkenwell Road, about 500 yards north of Barbican station (on the Circle and Metropolitan underground lines). Buses 4, 5 and 55 stop nearby. Car parking (afternoons) at Smithfield Market; or NCP Ltd, 158-70 Aldersgate St (01-606 7255)
2 **United Reformed Church History Society,** 86 Tavistock Place, WC1H 9RT (01-837 7661)
17 **Westminster Abbey Muniment Room and Library,** SW1 3PA (01-222 4233)
21 **Westminster City Libraries, Archives Department,** Victoria Library, Buckingham Palace Road, SW1W 9UD (01-730 7371)
19 **Westminster Diocesan Archives,** Archbishop's House, Ambrosden Avenue, SW1 1QJ (01-834 1964)
4 **Dr Williams's Library,** 14 Gordon Square, WC1H OAG (01-387 3727)

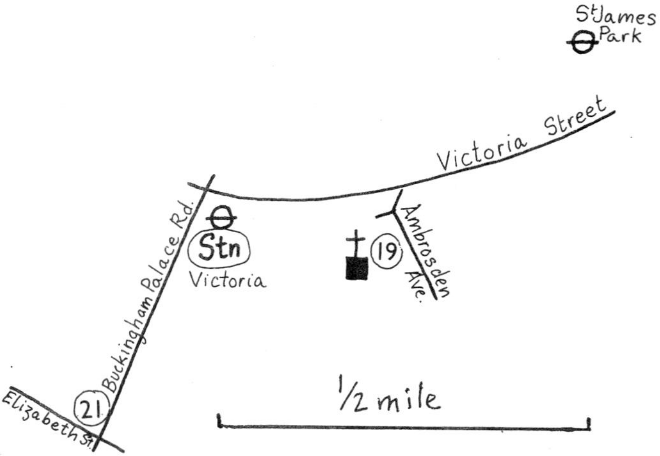

CENTRAL LONDON

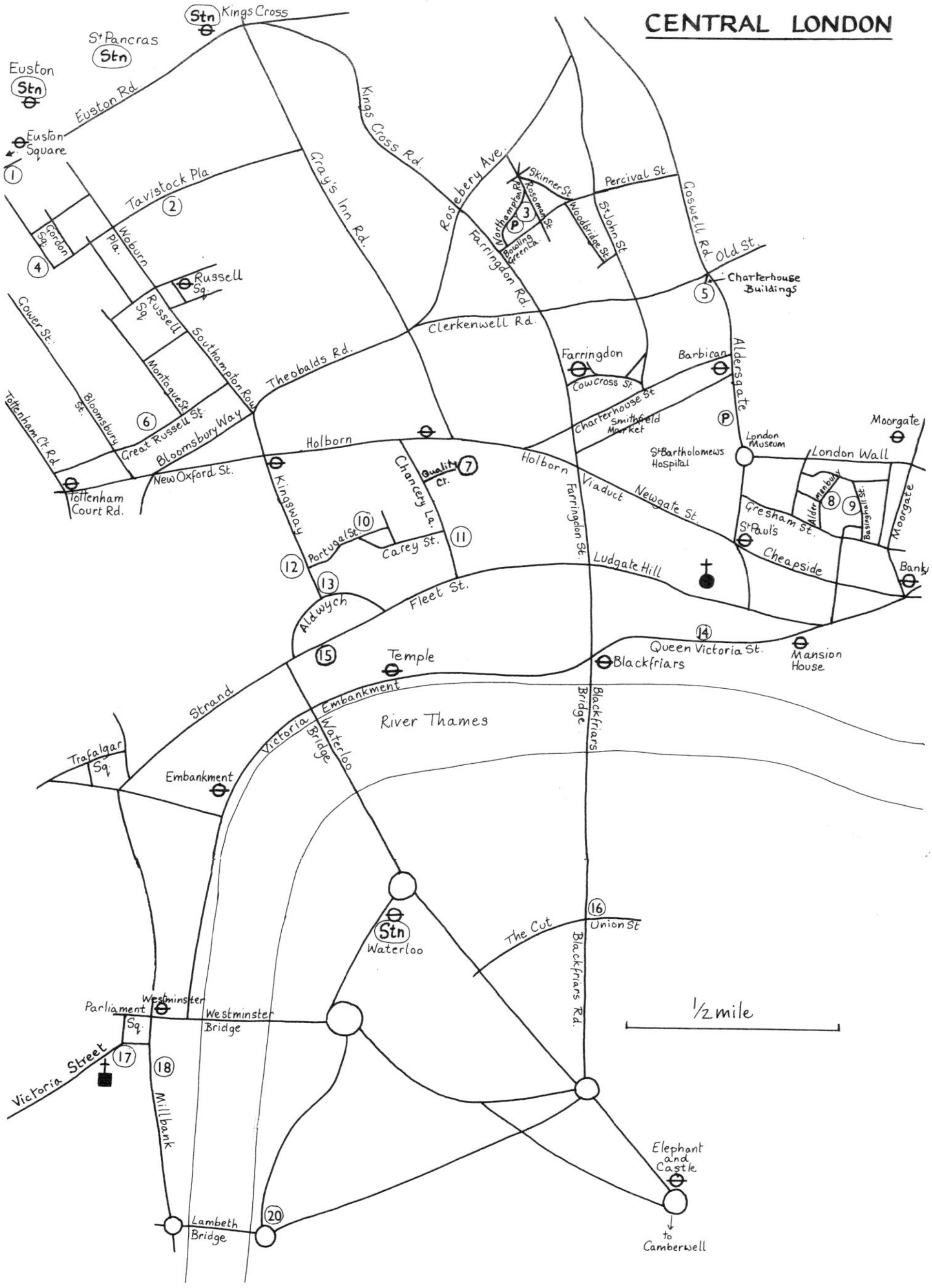

RECORD OFFICES IN ENGLAND AND WALES

This map shows ancient counties as they were before 19th and 20th century reorganization, particularly before the expansion of Greater London and also before the major re-drawing of county boundaries in 1974. County Record Offices of old counties are in capitals, and record offices holding bishop's transcripts and/or major probate records are underlined.

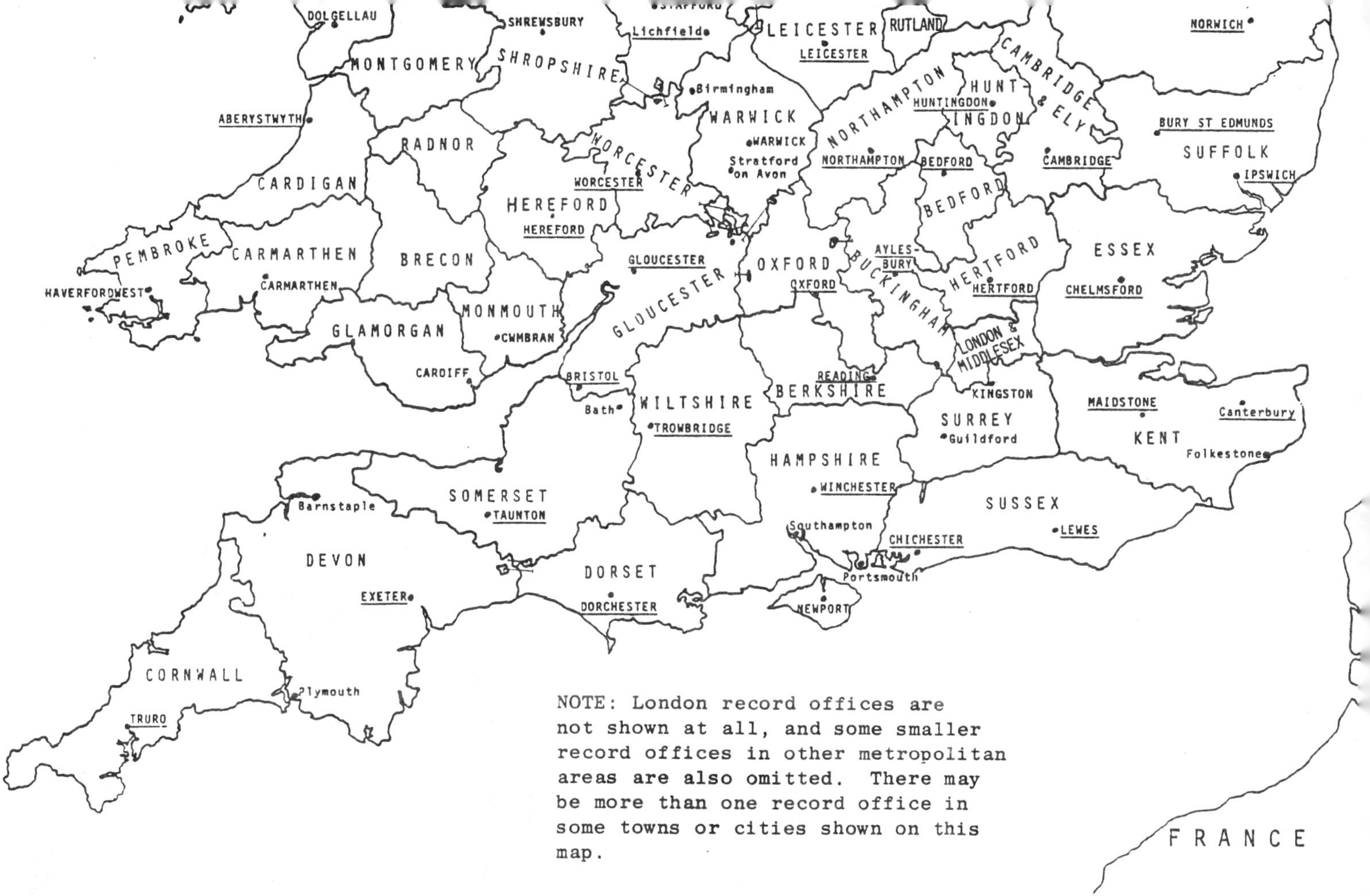

NOTE: London record offices are not shown at all, and some smaller record offices in other metropolitan areas are also omitted. There may be more than one record office in some towns or cities shown on this map.

London

Public Record Office,
Ruskin Avenue,
Kew, Richmond,
Surrey TW9 4DU
(01-876 3444)

If approaching from the north (Kew Bridge), Ruskin Avenue is about 20 yards beyond the railway bridge that crosses Mortlake Road.

KEW

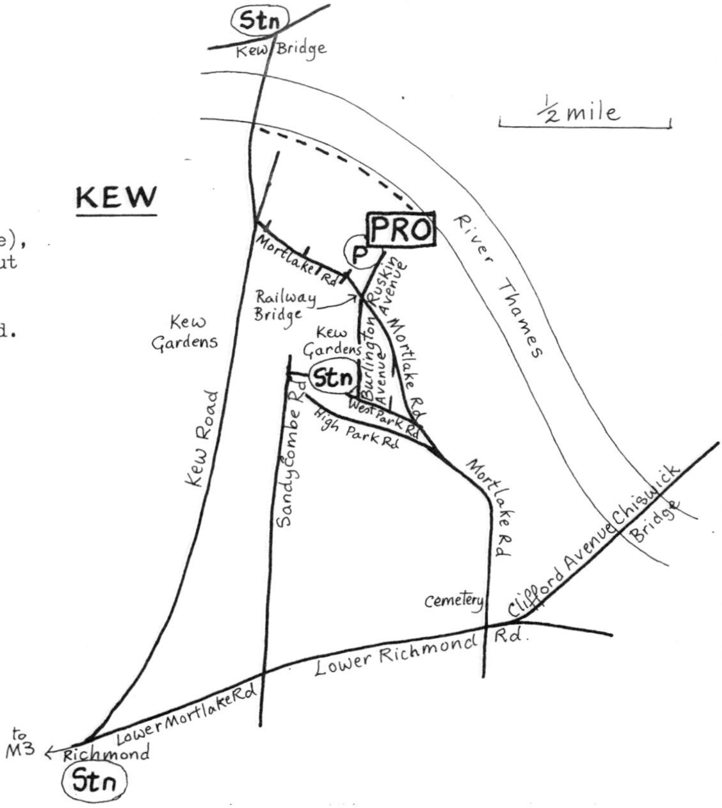

LAMBETH & CAMBERWELL

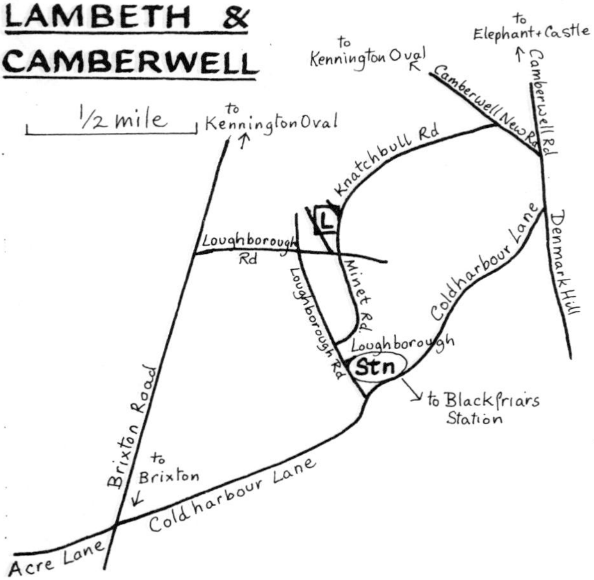

Lambeth Archives Department,
Minet Library,
52 Knatchbull Road,
London SE5 9QY
(01-733 3279)

Greater Manchester

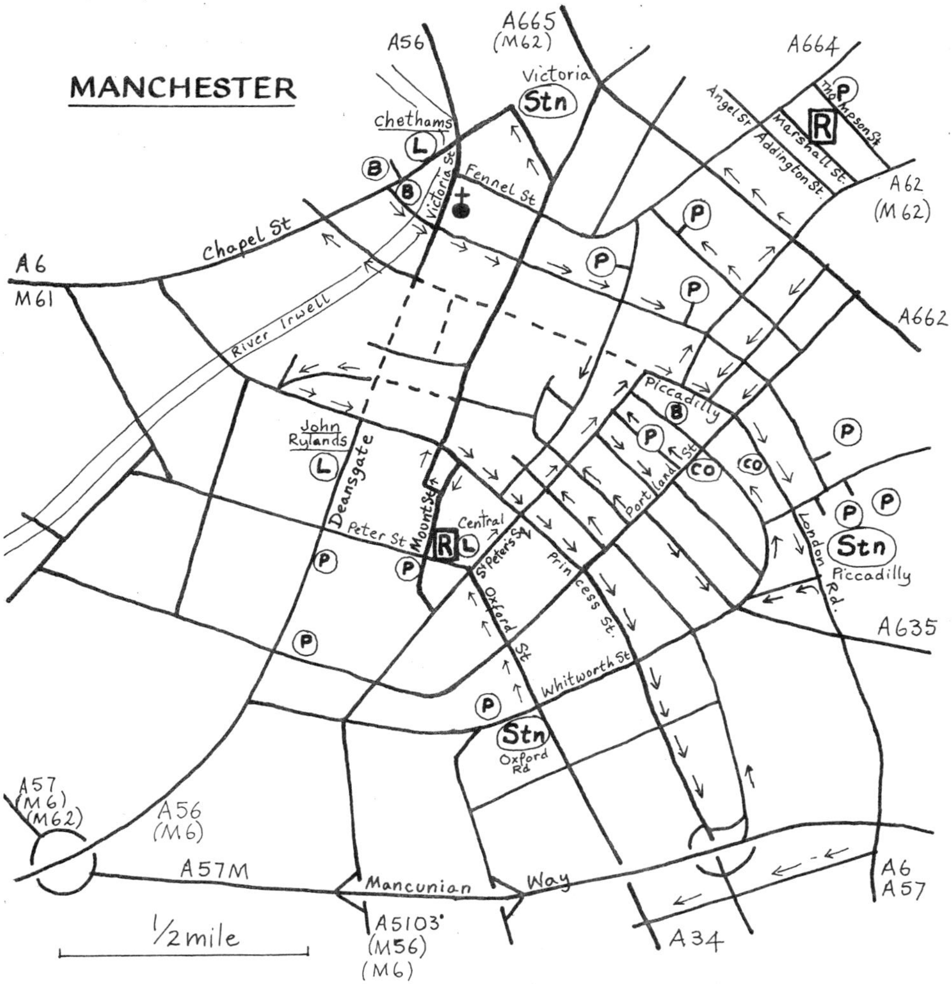

Greater Manchester Record Office,
56 Marshall Street,
New Cross, Ancoats,
Manchester M4 5FU
(061-247 3383/3893)

Manchester Central Library, Archives Department, St Peter's Square,
Manchester M2 5PD
(061-236 9422 ext 269)

John Rylands University Library of Manchester, Deansgate, Manchester
M3 3EH (061-834 5343)

Not mapped:

Bolton Metropolitan Borough Archives,
Central Library, Le Mans Crescent,
Bolton BL1 1SA (0204 22311 ext 318);

Stockport Library of Local Studies,
Central Library, Wellington Road South,
Stockport SK13 3RS (061-480 2966/3038);

Wigan Record Office, Town Hall,
Leigh WN7 2DY (0942 672421 ext 65/6).

Greater Manchester

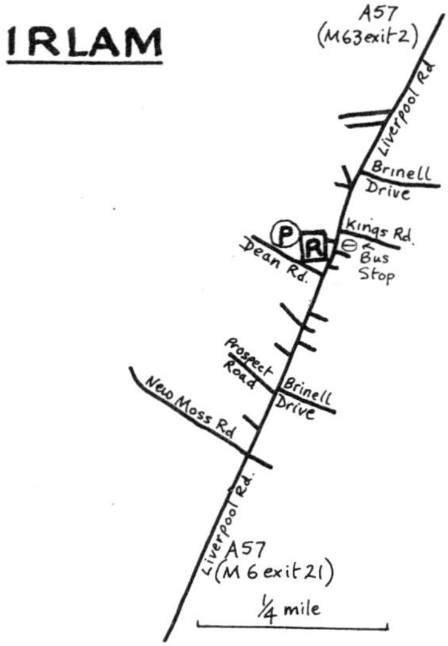

Salford Archives Centre,
658/662 Liverpool Road,
Irlam,
Manchester M30 5AD
(061-775 5643)

"Genealogical Sources in the City of Salford"

R...Record Office
CO...County Offices
L...Library
M...Museum
P...Car Park
B...Bus Station
Stn..Railway Station
----.Foot route

Merseyside

Merseyside County Archives Service, 64-66 Islington, Liverpool (051-207 3697)

Liverpool Record Office,
Brown, Picton and Hornby Libraries,
William Brown Street,
Liverpool L3 8EW
(051-207 2147)

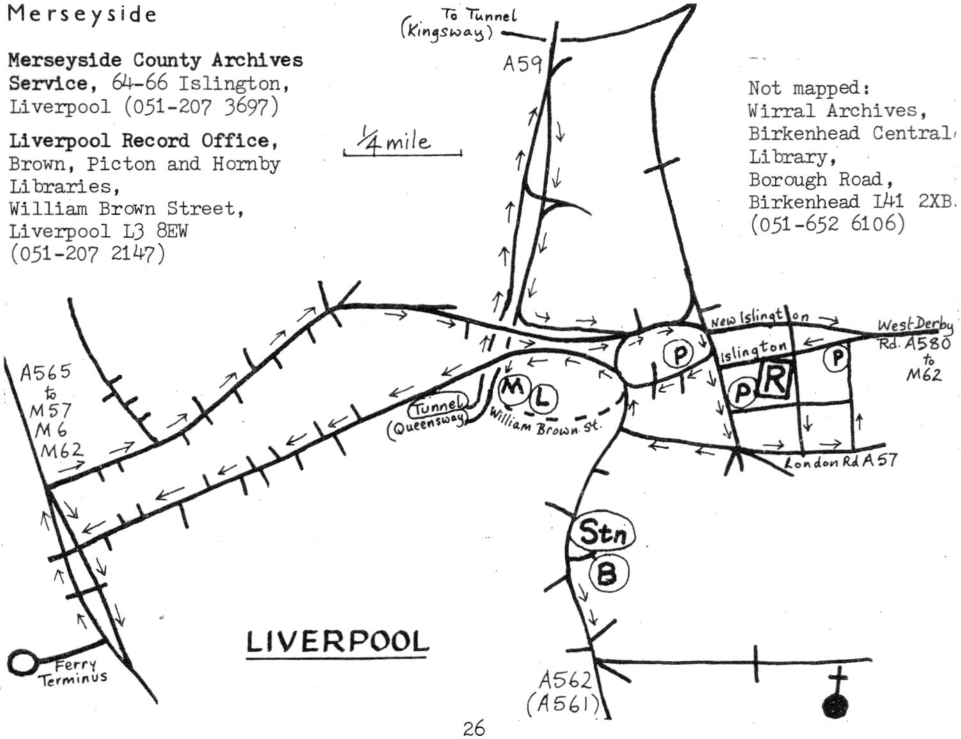

Not mapped:
Wirral Archives,
Birkenhead Central Library,
Borough Road,
Birkenhead L41 2XB.
(051-652 6106)

Birmingham Reference Library,
Birmingham B3 3HQ (021-235 4219)

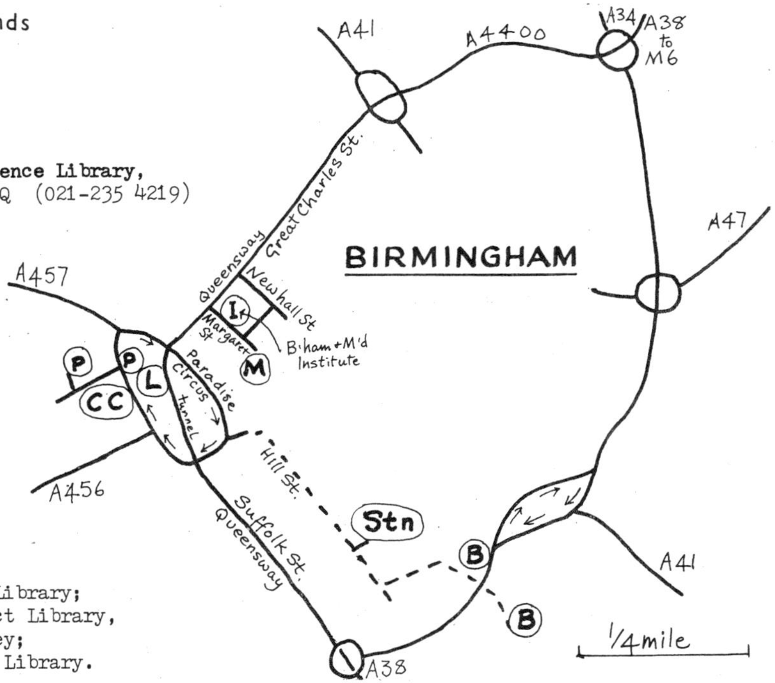

Not mapped:
Dudley Central Library;
Sandwell District Library, Smethwick, Warley;
Walsall Central Library.

Coventry City Record Office,
Room 220 (second floor),
Broadgate House,
Broadgate,
Coventry CV1 1NG
(0203 25555 ext 2768)

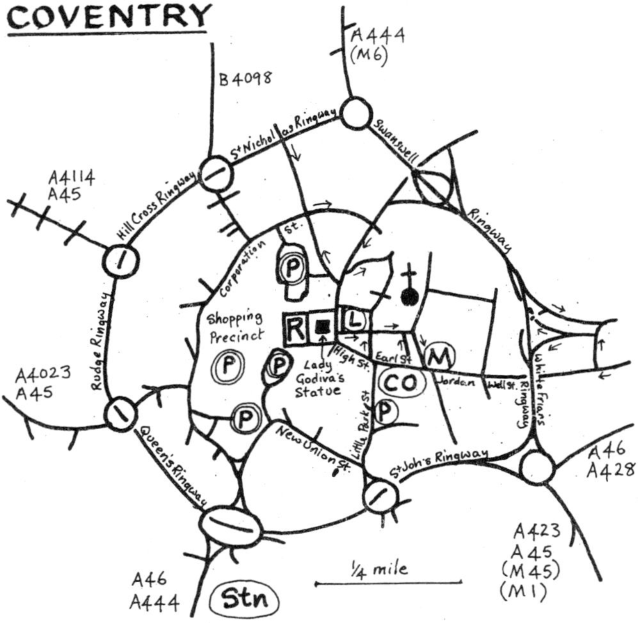

Norfolk

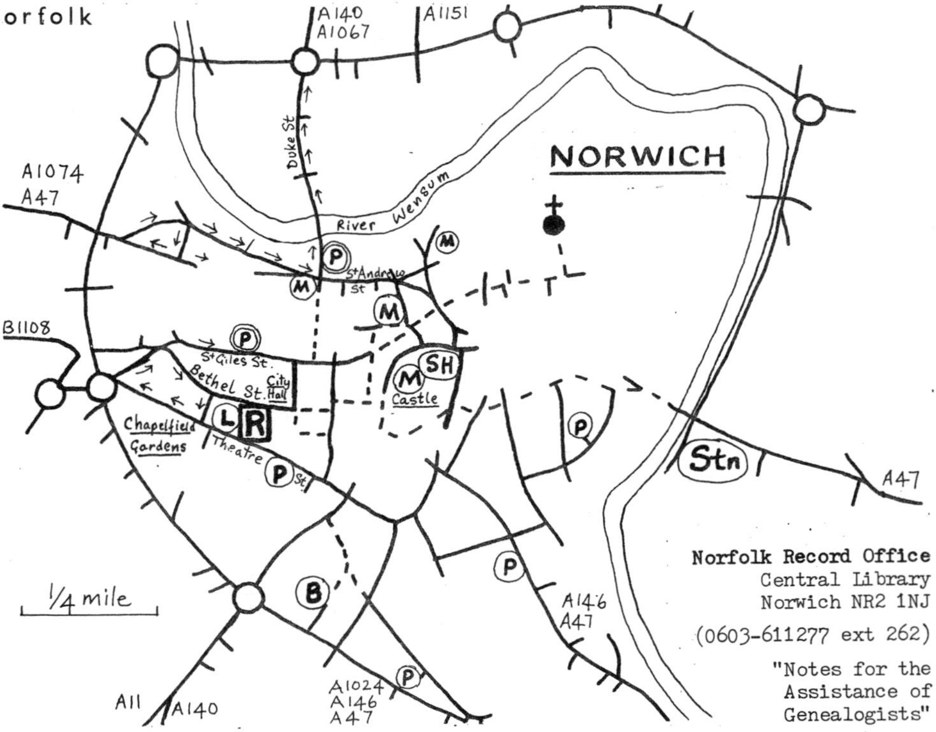

Norfolk Record Office
Central Library
Norwich NR2 1NJ
(0603-611277 ext 262)

"Notes for the Assistance of Genealogists"

Northamptonshire

Northamptonshire Record Office,
Delapré Abbey, Northampton NN4 9AW
(0604 62129)

The record office is in a country house in parkland on the outskirts of Northampton, about a mile from the town centre.

Northampton Central Library,
Abington Street, Northampton NN1 2BA
(0604 34833)

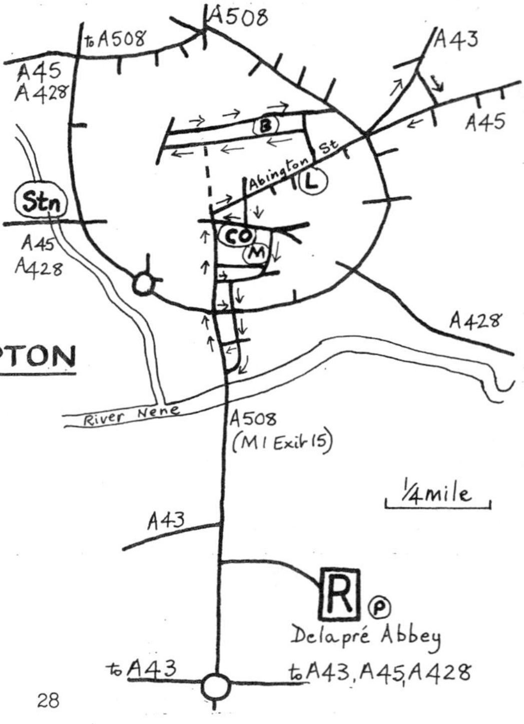

R ... Record Office
CO ... County Offices
L ... Library
M ... Museum
P ... Car Park
B ... Bus Station
Stn .. Railway Station
- - - - Foot route

Northumberland

Northumberland Record Office,
Melton Park, North Gosforth,
Newcastle upon Tyne NE3 5QX
(Wideopen (0632) 362680)

Tyneside PTE buses (yellow):
44, 45 to Melton Park;
46 to Polwarth Drive.

"Genealogical Sources List", 15p

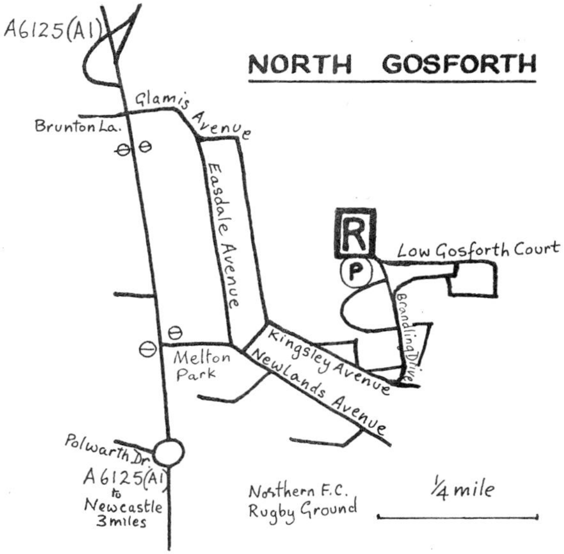

Nottinghamshire

Nottinghamshire Record Office,
County House, High Pavement,
Nottingham NG1 1HR (0602 504524)

Not mapped:
Nottingham
University
Manuscripts
Department,
University
Library,
University
Park,
Nottingham
NG7 2RD
(0602 56101
ext 3437)

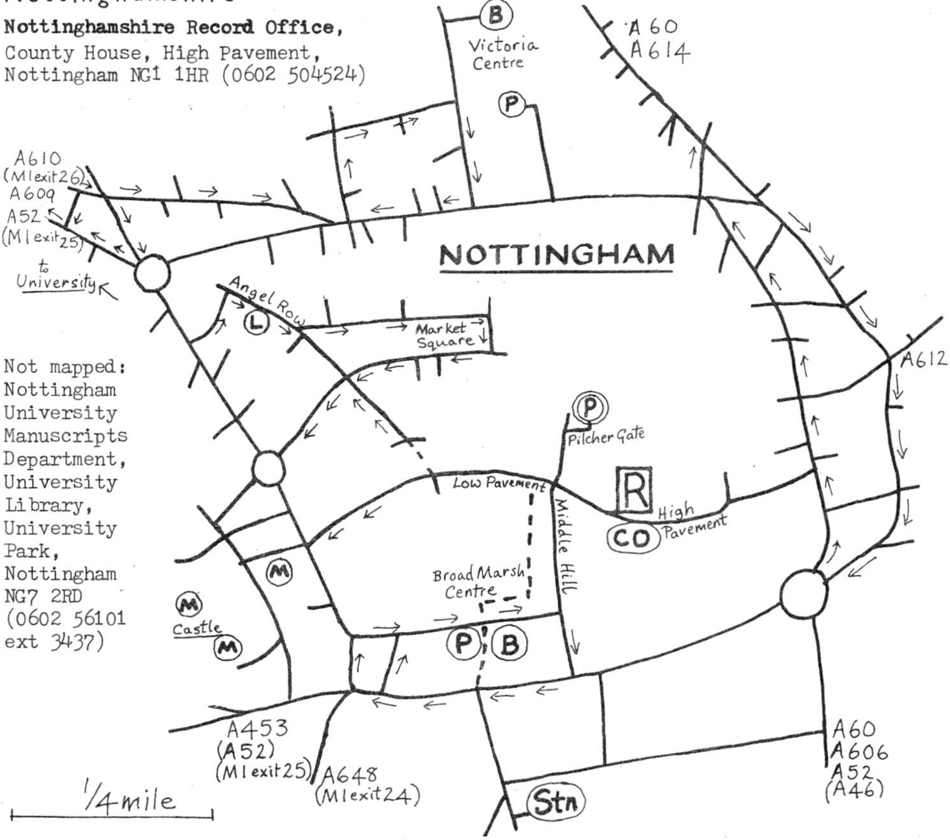

Oxfordshire

Park and Ride bus system operates on A34 approach from north and south

Bodleian Library, Department of Western Manuscripts,
Oxford OX1 3BG (0865 244675)
(reader's ticket necessary; daily charge; parish and probate records now at County Record Office)

OXFORD

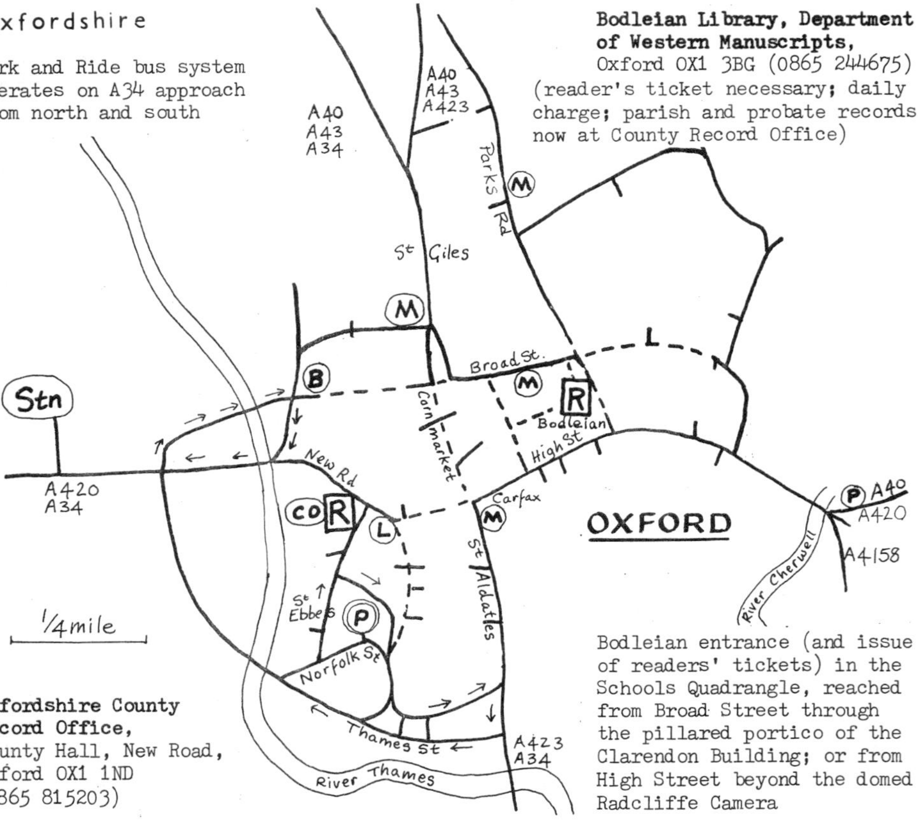

Oxfordshire County Record Office,
County Hall, New Road,
Oxford OX1 1ND
(0865 815203)

Bodleian entrance (and issue of readers' tickets) in the Schools Quadrangle, reached from Broad Street through the pillared portico of the Clarendon Building; or from High Street beyond the domed Radcliffe Camera

Shropshire

SHREWSBURY

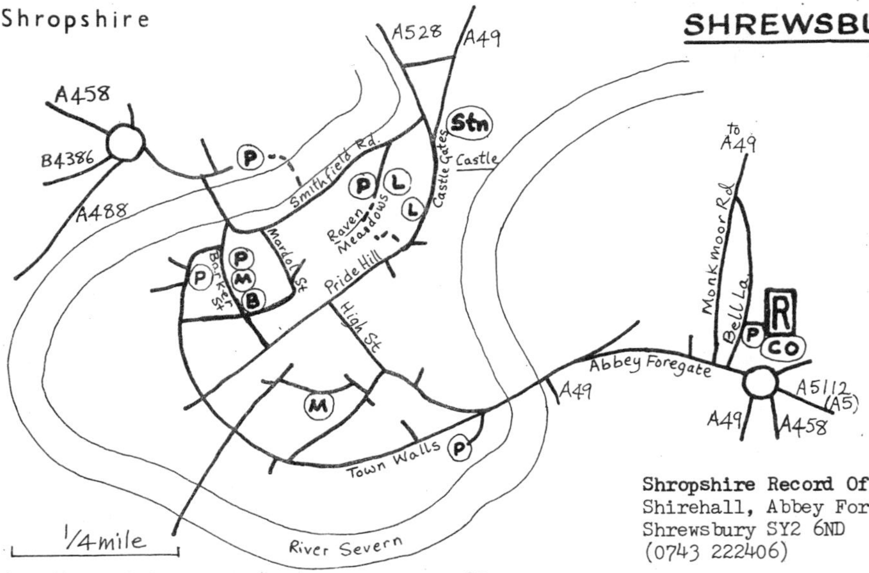

Shropshire Record Office,
Shirehall, Abbey Foregate,
Shrewsbury SY2 6ND
(0743 222406)

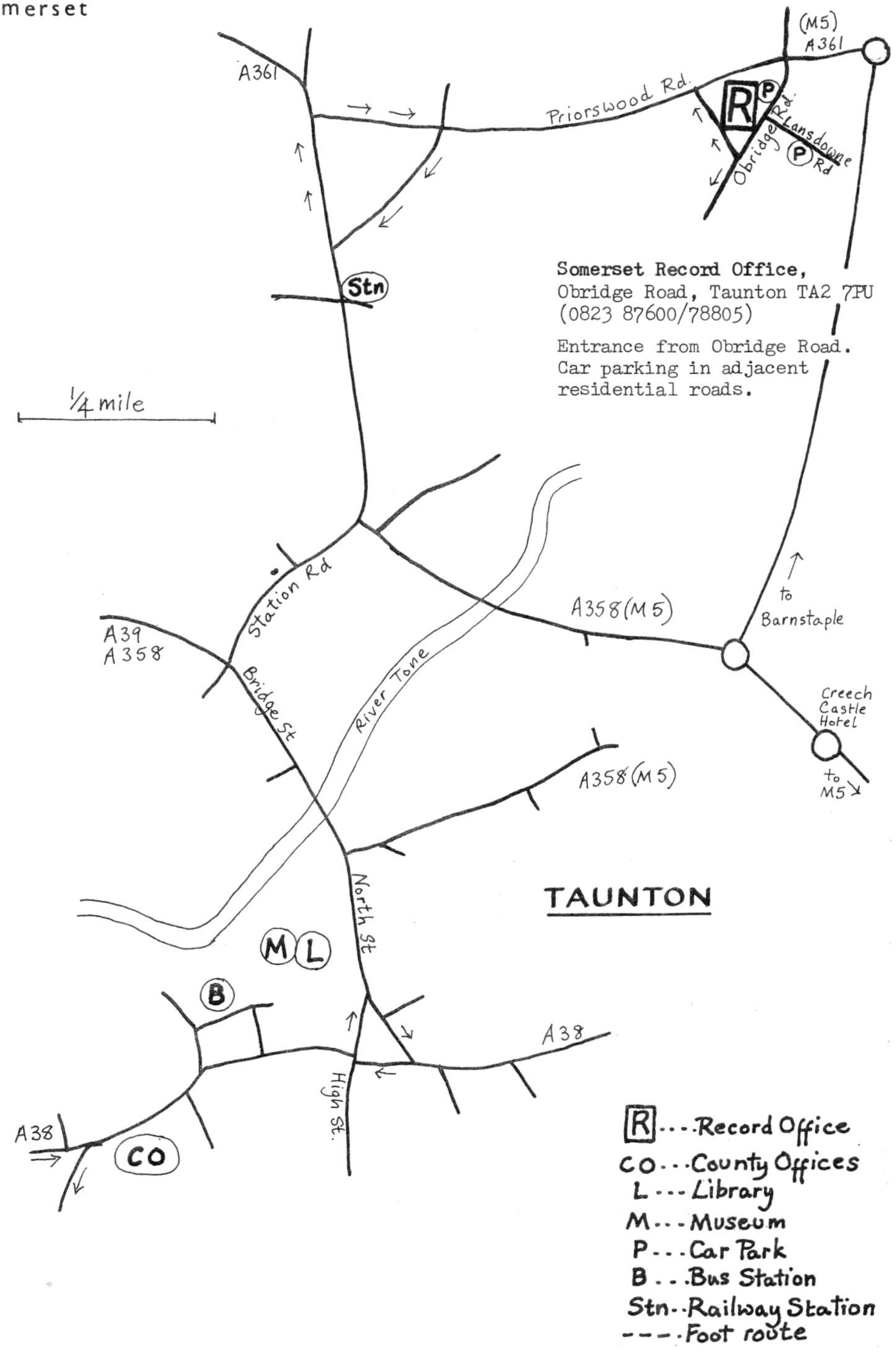

Somerset Record Office,
Obridge Road, Taunton TA2 7PU
(0823 87600/78805)

Entrance from Obridge Road.
Car parking in adjacent residential roads.

Staffordshire

Staffordshire Record Office,
County Buildings,
Eastgate Street,
Stafford ST16 2LZ
(0785 3121 ext 7910)

William Salt Library,
Eastgate Street
(adjacent to the record office)
(0785 52276)

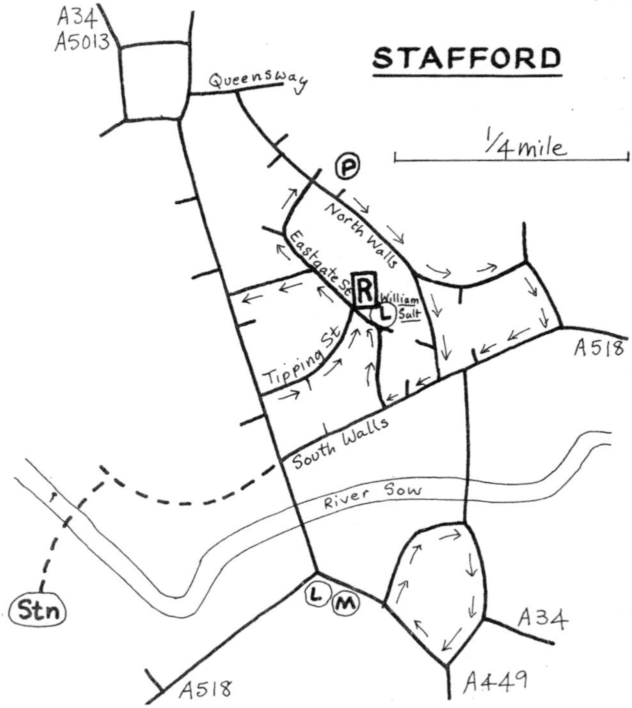

R . . . Record Office
CO . . . County Offices
L . . . Library
M . . . Museum
P . . . Car Park
B . . . Bus Station
Stn . . Railway Station
- - - . Foot route

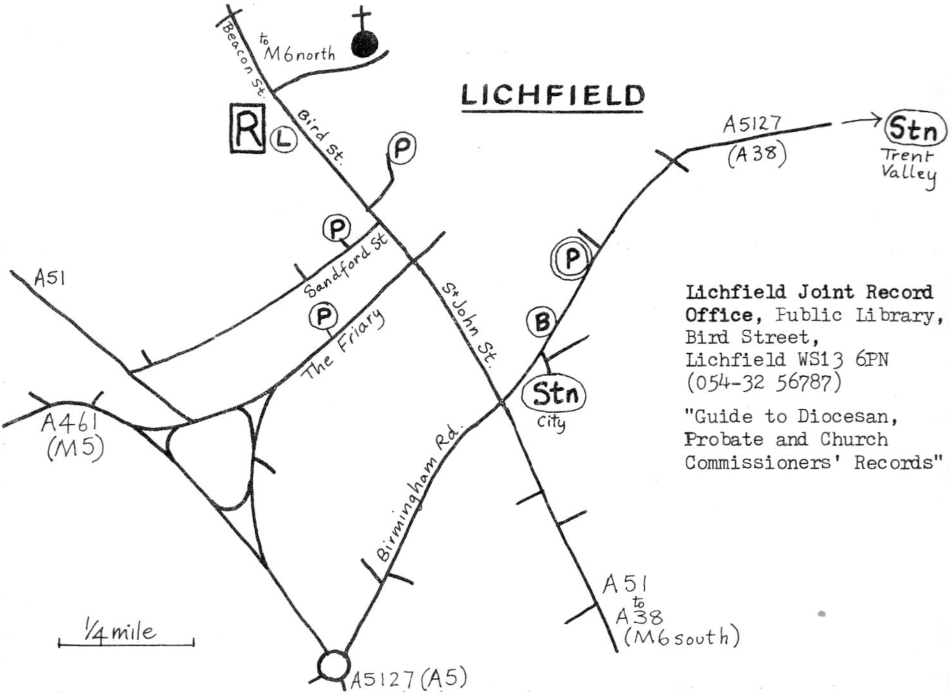

Lichfield Joint Record Office, Public Library,
Bird Street,
Lichfield WS13 6PN
(054-32 56787)

"Guide to Diocesan, Probate and Church Commissioners' Records"

Suffolk

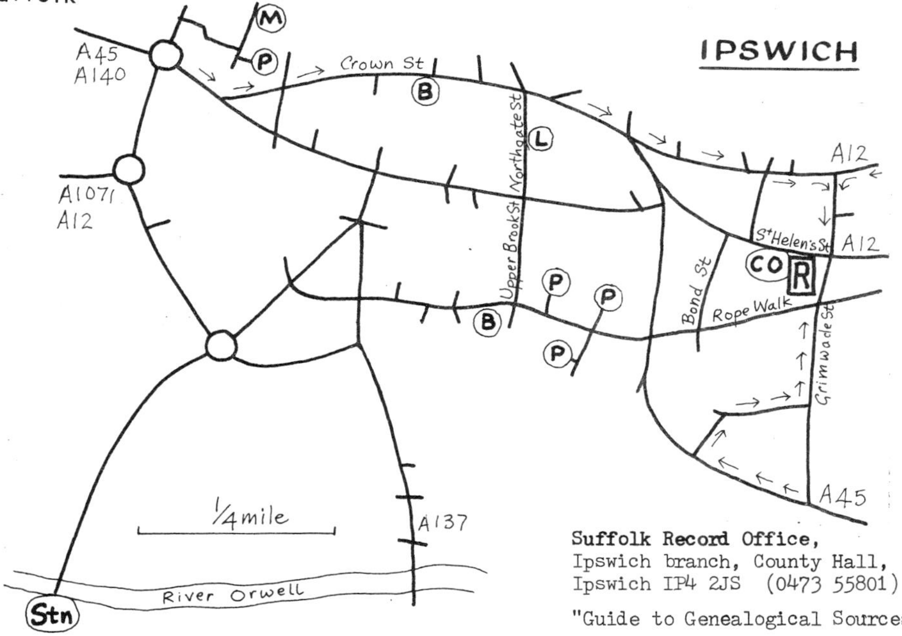

Suffolk Record Office,
Ipswich branch, County Hall,
Ipswich IP4 2JS (0473 55801)

"Guide to Genealogical Sources"

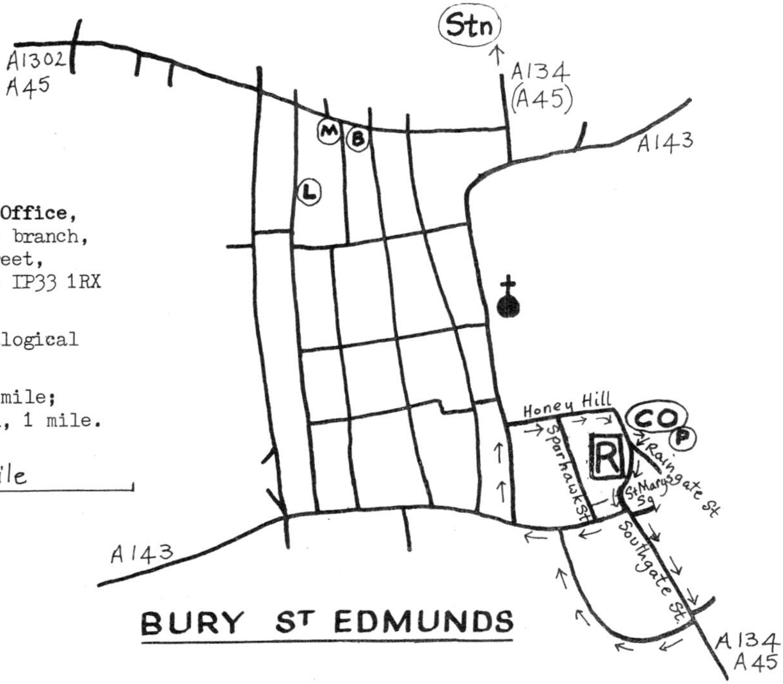

Suffolk Record Office,
Bury St Edmunds branch,
School Hall Street,
Bury St Edmunds IP33 1RX
(0284 63143)

"Guide to Genealogical Sources"

Bus station, $\frac{3}{4}$ mile;
Railway station, 1 mile.

1/4 mile

Surrey

Surrey Record Office,
County Hall,
Penrhyn Road,
Kingston upon Thames
KT1 2DN
(01-546 1050 ext 3561)

Restricted car parking only.

Buses 281 and 211 from Surbiton Station to County Hall.

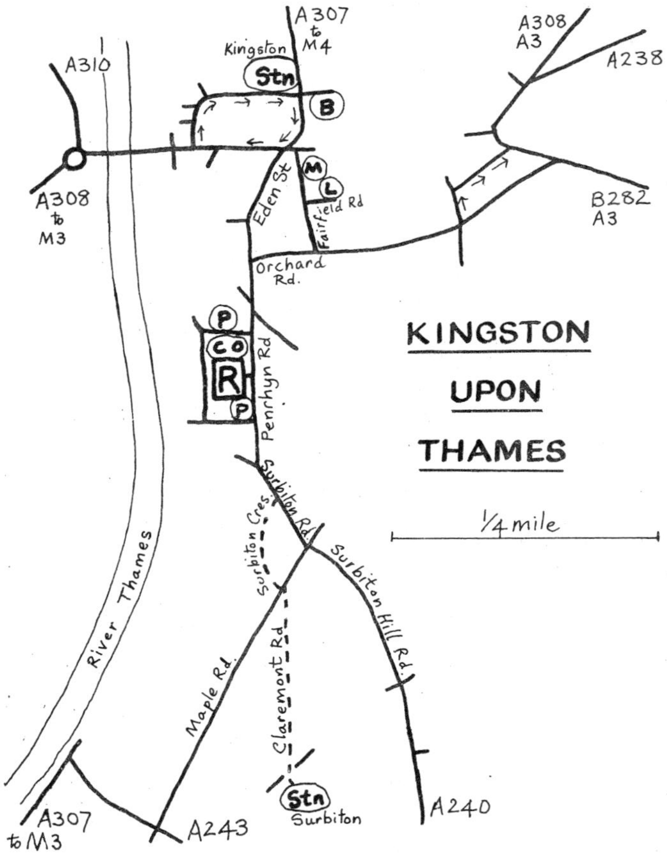

R....Record Office
CO...County Offices
L...Library
M...Museum
P...Car Park
B...Bus Station
Stn..Railway Station
----Foot route

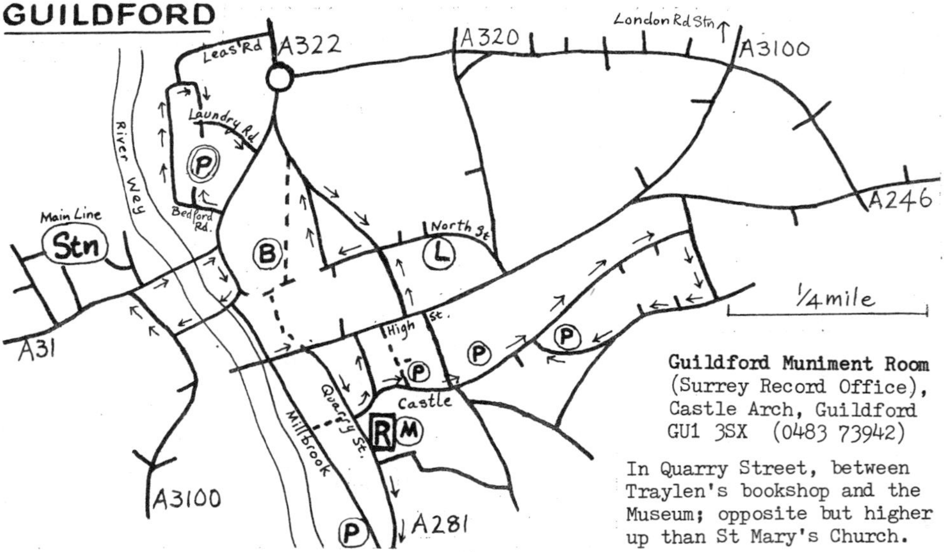

Guildford Muniment Room
(Surrey Record Office),
Castle Arch, Guildford
GU1 3SX (0483 73942)

In Quarry Street, between Traylen's bookshop and the Museum; opposite but higher up than St Mary's Church.

East Sussex

SAS = Sussex Archaeological Society, Barbican House, Lewes BN7 1YE (079-16 4379)

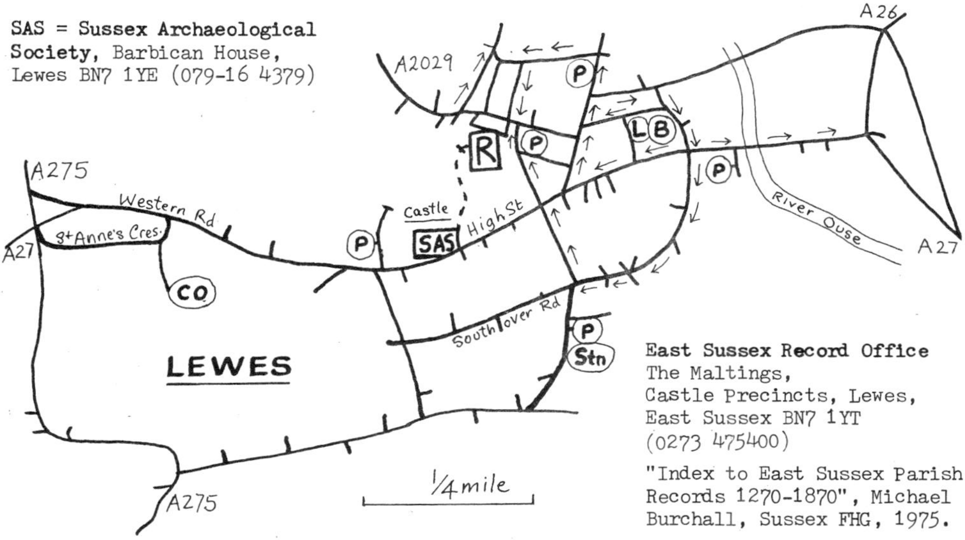

East Sussex Record Office
The Maltings,
Castle Precincts, Lewes,
East Sussex BN7 1YT
(0273 475400)

"Index to East Sussex Parish Records 1270-1870", Michael Burchall, Sussex FHG, 1975.

Pedestrian access to The Maltings from the High Street is via the Castle Gate (through the Barbican Arch and past the Bowling Green).

Parking there is restricted to deliveries and disabled drivers; the nearest street parking is off the Offham Road (A2029) (about 5 minutes' walk), or use North Street pay car park.

West Sussex

West Sussex Record Office,
John Edes' House,
West Street,
Chichester PO19 1RN
(0243 785100 ext 2770)

"Genealogists' Guide to the West Sussex Record Office", Peter M. Wilkinson, 1979.

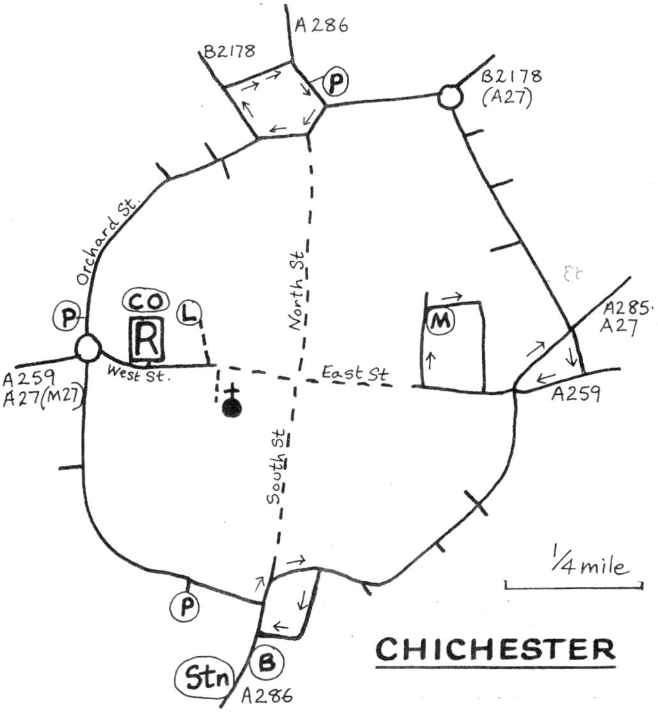

Tyne and Wear

Tyne and Wear Archives Department, Blandford House, West Blandford Street, Newcastle upon Tyne NE1 4JA (0632 326789)

For Northumberland Record Office, North Gosforth, see page 25

Not mapped:
Tyne and Wear Archives Department (North Shields), Local Studies Centre, Howard Street, North Shields NE30 1LY (089-45 82811);
Gateshead Central Library, Prince Consort Road, Gateshead NE8 4LN (0632 773478)

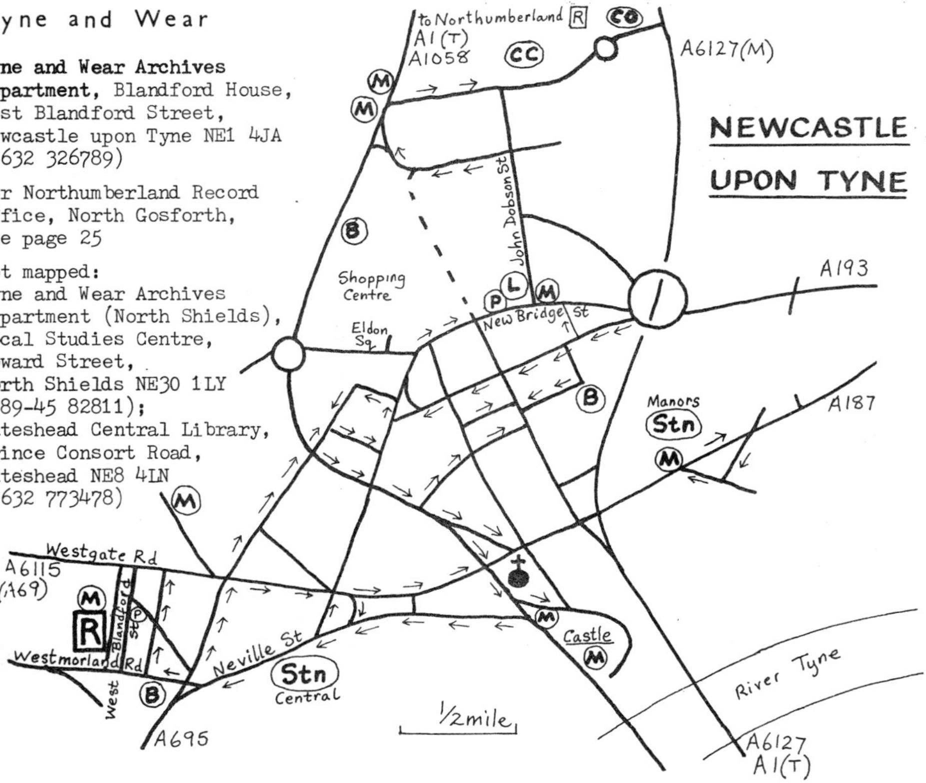

Isle of Wight

Isle of Wight Record Office, 26 Hillside, Newport, Isle of Wight PO30 2EB (0983 524031 ext 132)

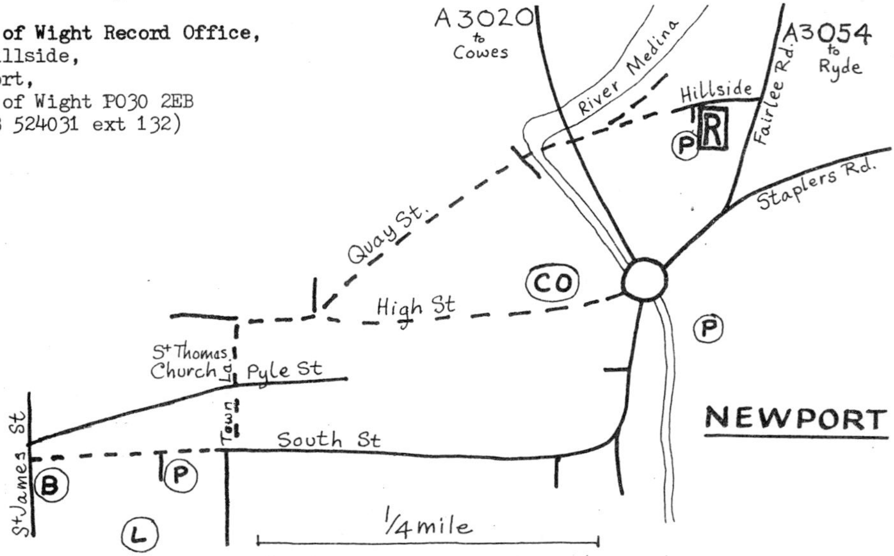

Warwickshire

Warwick County Record Office,
Priory Park, Cape Road,
Warwick CV34 4JS
(0926 493431 ext 2508)

"Tracing your Ancestors in Warwickshire", F.C. Markwell, BMSGH, 1981.

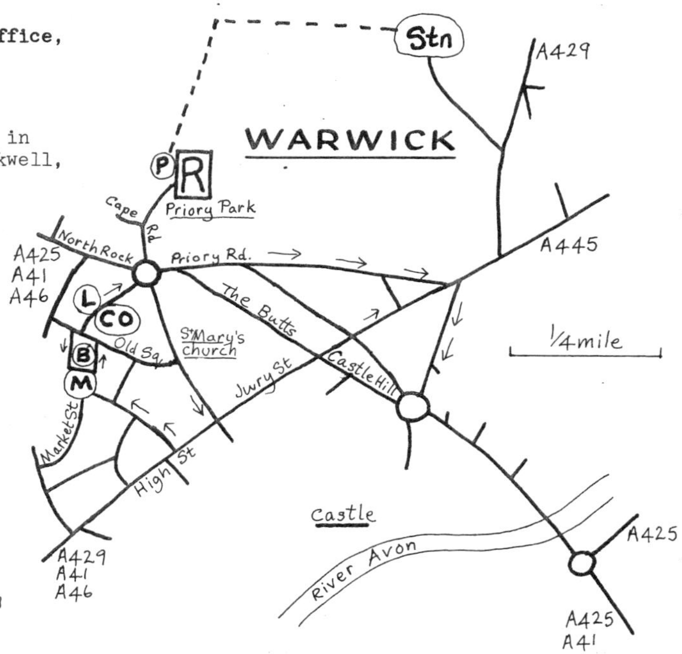

R ... Record Office
CO ... County Offices
L ... Library
M ... Museum
P ... Car Park
B ... Bus Station
Stn .. Railway Station
- - - . Foot route

The Shakespeare Birthplace Trust Record Office,
Guild Street,
Stratford upon Avon CV37 6QW
(0789 204016)

Entrance from Guild Street

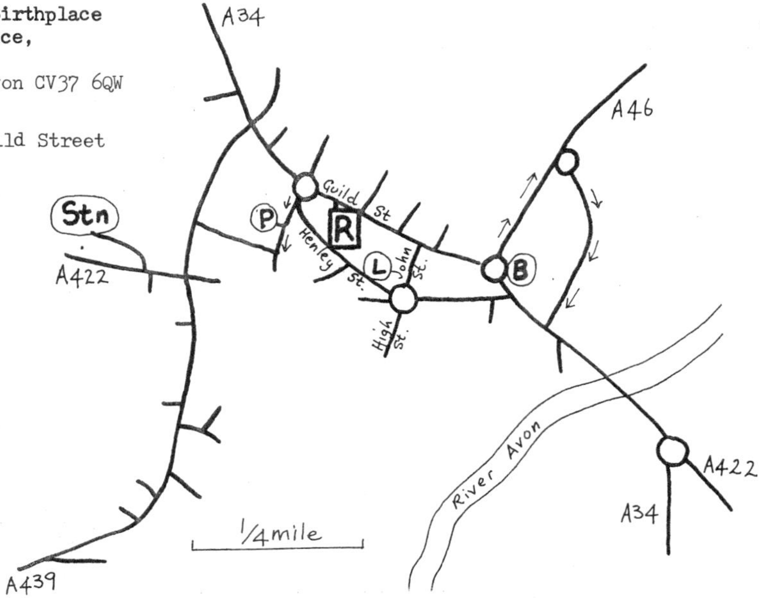

STRATFORD UPON AVON

Wiltshire

Wiltshire Record Office,
County Hall,
Trowbridge BA14 8JG
(022-14 3641)

"Sources for the History of a Wiltshire Family" (1981)

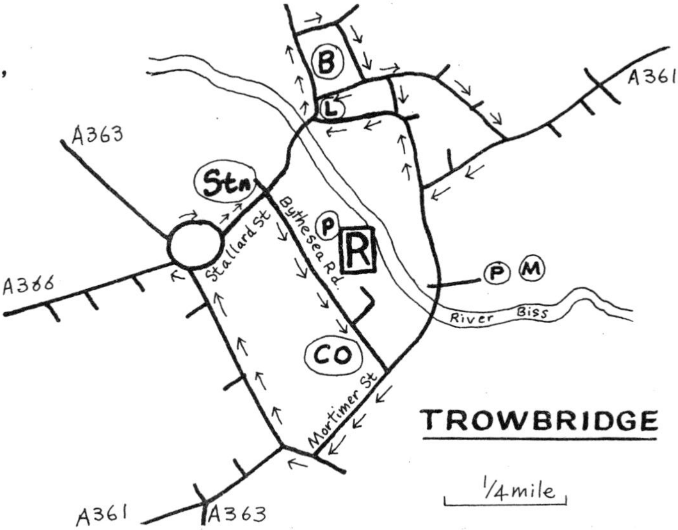

North Yorkshire

North Yorkshire County Record Office,
County Hall,
Northallerton,
North Yorks DL7 8SG
(0609 3123 ext 455)

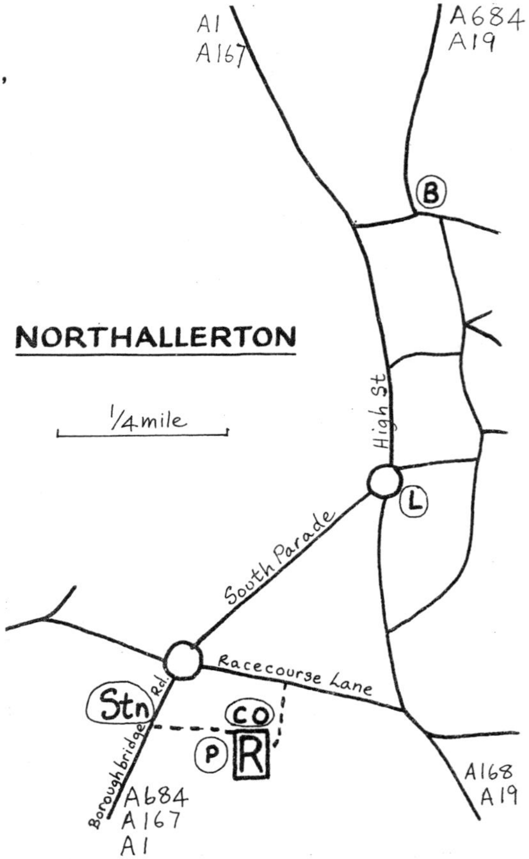

R ... Record Office
CO ... County Offices
L ... Library
M ... Museum
P ... Car Park
B ... Bus Station
Stn .. Railway Station
---- . Foot route

North Yorkshire

North Yorkshire Record Office, The York Archives, Exhibition Square, York (0904 51533)

Accessible **only** from Exhibition Square itself. Part of York City Art Gallery building.

"A Guide to Genealogical Sources in the Borthwick Institute of Historical Research", C.C. Webb, 1981

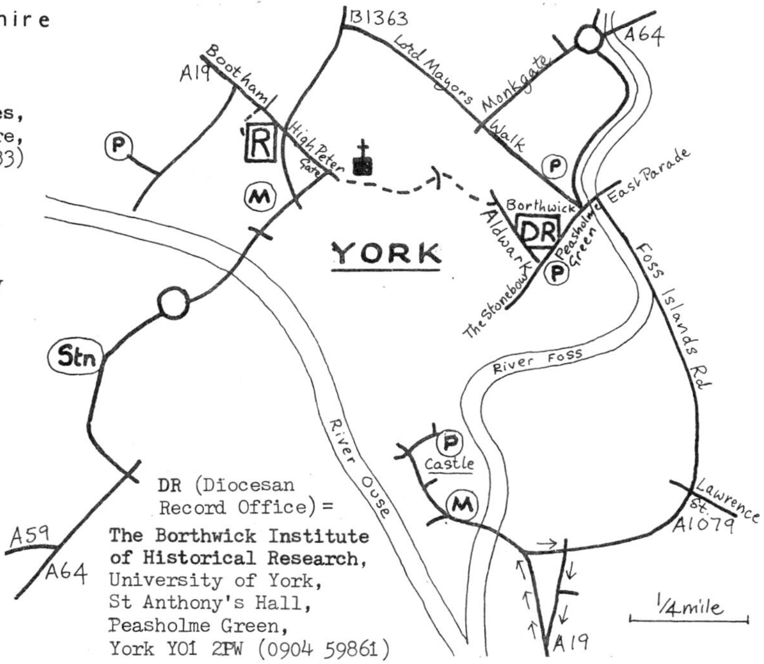

DR (Diocesan Record Office) = **The Borthwick Institute of Historical Research,** University of York, St Anthony's Hall, Peasholme Green, York YO1 2PW (0904 59861)

South Yorkshire

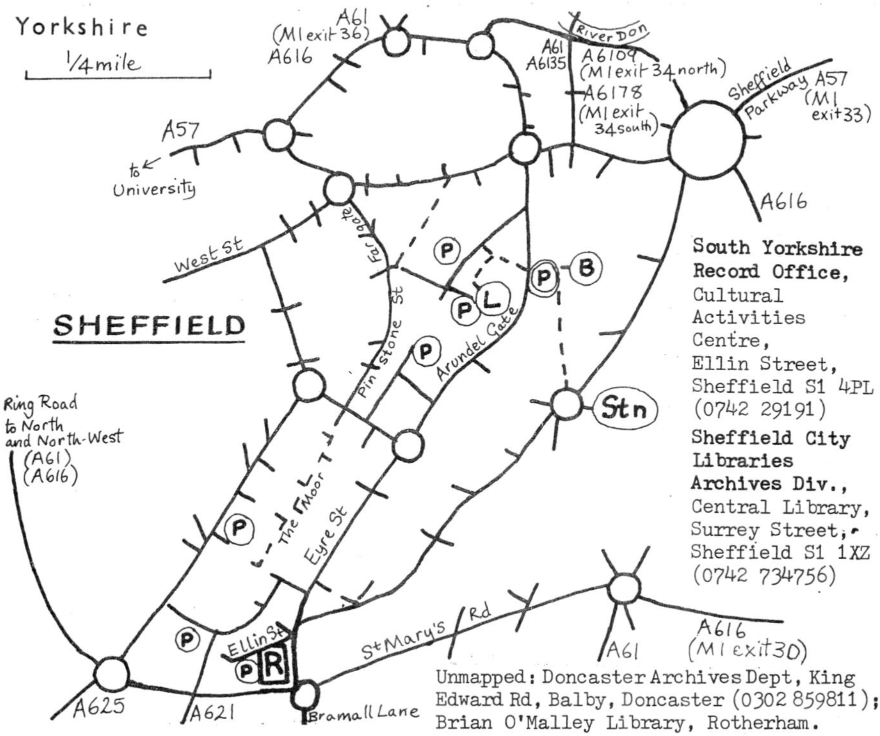

South Yorkshire Record Office, Cultural Activities Centre, Ellin Street, Sheffield S1 4PL (0742 29191)

Sheffield City Libraries Archives Div., Central Library, Surrey Street, Sheffield S1 1XZ (0742 734756)

Unmapped: Doncaster Archives Dept, King Edward Rd, Balby, Doncaster (0302 859811); Brian O'Malley Library, Rotherham.

West Yorkshire

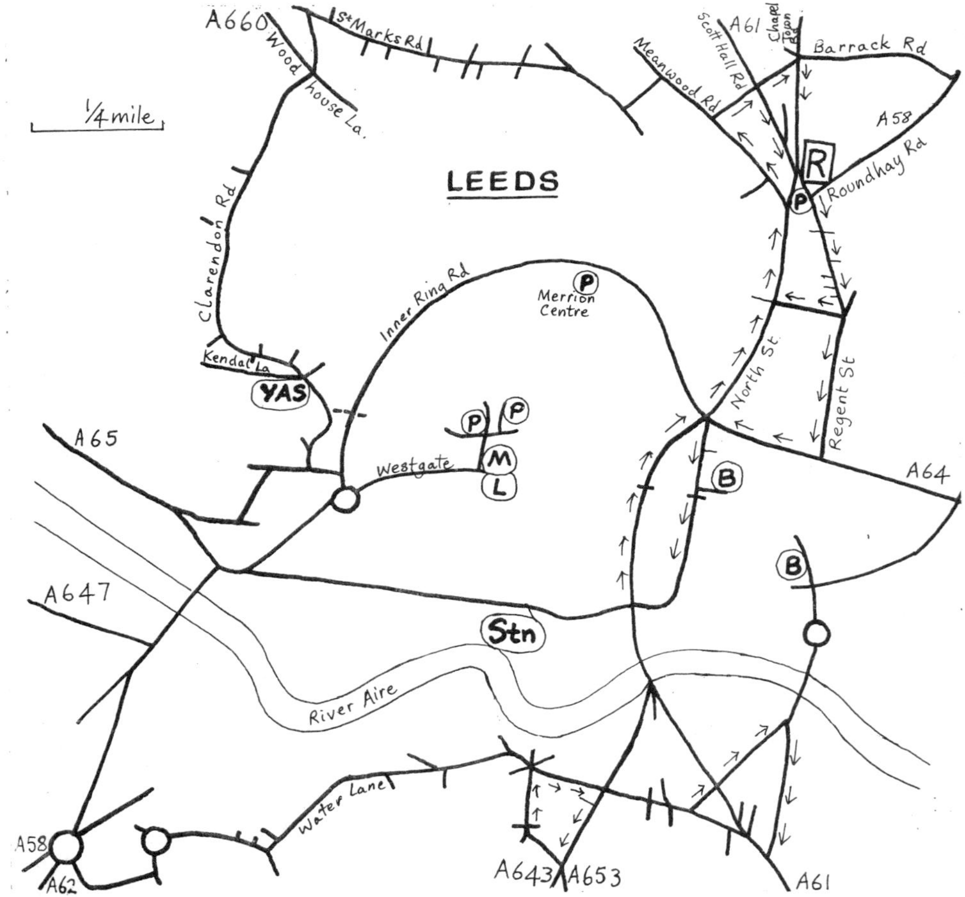

West Yorkshire Archive Service:

Leeds District Archives,
Chapeltown Road, Sheepscar,
Leeds LS7 3AP (0532 628339)

Yorkshire Archaeological Society,
Claremont, Clarendon Road,
Leeds LS2 9NZ (0532 456362)

Not mapped:
Bradford Archives Department, Central Library,
Prince's Way, Bradford BD1 1NN (0274 753683)
Calderdale Archives Department, Central Library,
Northgate House, Northgate, Halifax HX1 1UN
(0422 57257 ext 2636)
Kirklees Archives Department, Central Library,
Princess Alexandra Walk, Huddersfield HD2 2SU
(0484 513808 ext 207)

R ... Record Office
CO ... County Offices
L ... Library
M ... Museum
P ... Car Park
B ... Bus Station
Stn .. Railway Station
---- Foot route

West Yorkshire

West Yorkshire Archive Service HQ, Registry of Deeds, Newstead Rd., Wakefield WF1 2DE (0924 367111 ext 2352)

Wakefield Metropolitan District Archives (incl. Pontefract Corporation), Principal Local Studies Officer, Wakefield District Library HQ, Blane Lane, Wakefield WF2 0DQ (0924 371231)

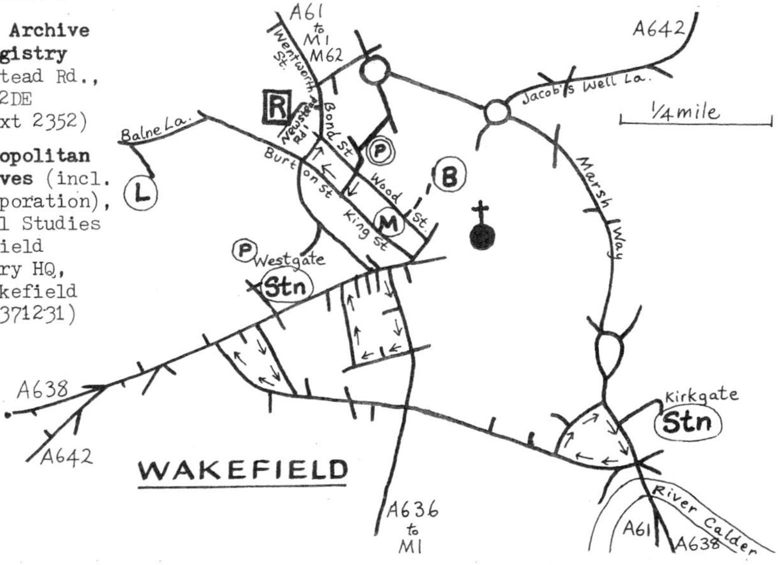

WALES

Clwyd

Clwyd Record Office, 46 Clwyd Street, Ruthin LL15 1HP (08242 3077)

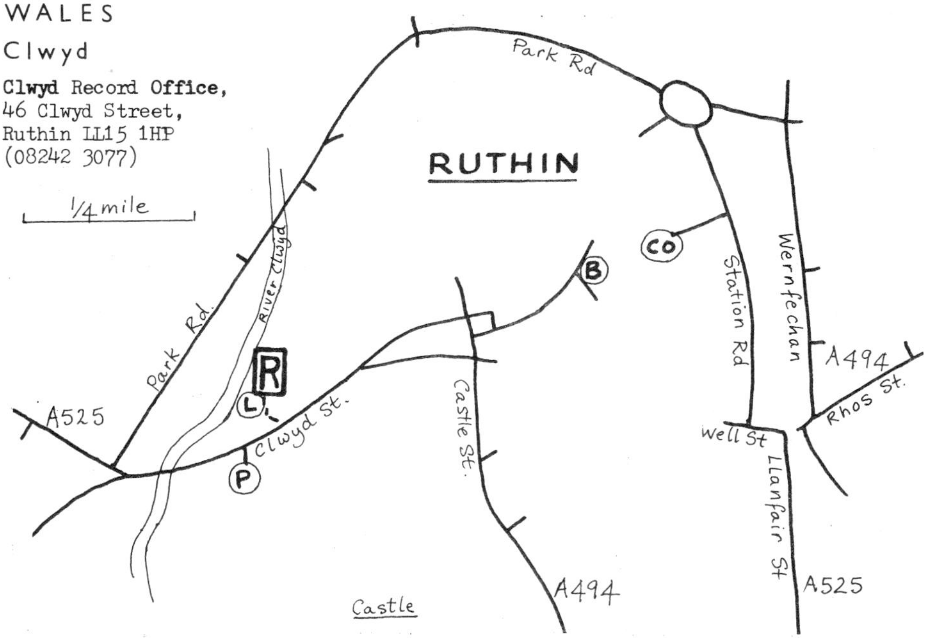

Not mapped:
Clwyd Record Office, The Old Rectory, Hawarden, Deeside CH5 3NR (0244 532364).

The Record Office (and Library) are at the end of Rectory Lane, which turns off the main A55 road opposite the junction with A550 (from Wrexham and the south). From the railway station it is about a quarter of a mile (east) along Station Road and the main A55, beyond the A550 (north) junction (war memorial) and Church Lane.

National Library of Wales (N.L.W.),
Aberystwyth, Dyfed SY23 3BU
(0970 3816)

Dyfed Archives,
Ceredigion Record Office,
Aberystwyth
(0970 617581)

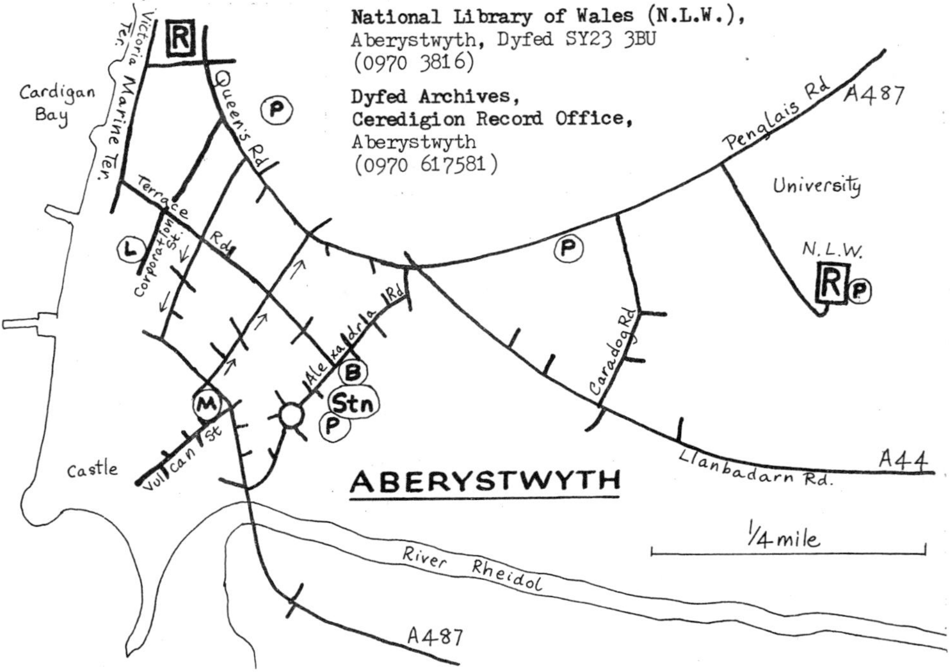

Dyfed Archive Service,
Carmarthenshire Record Office,
County Hall,
Carmarthen SA31 1JP
(0267 4251)

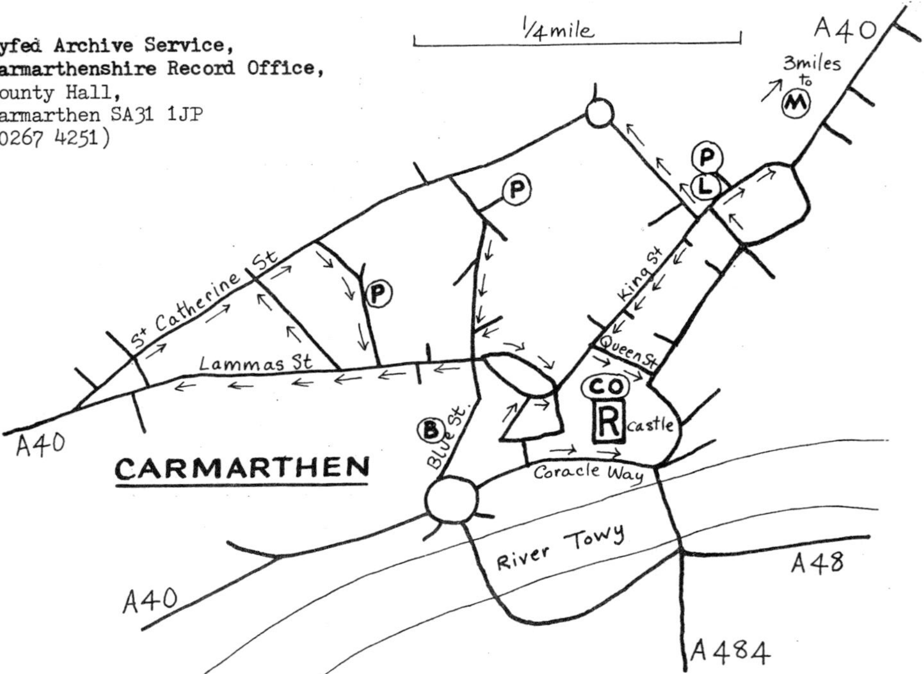

Dyfed

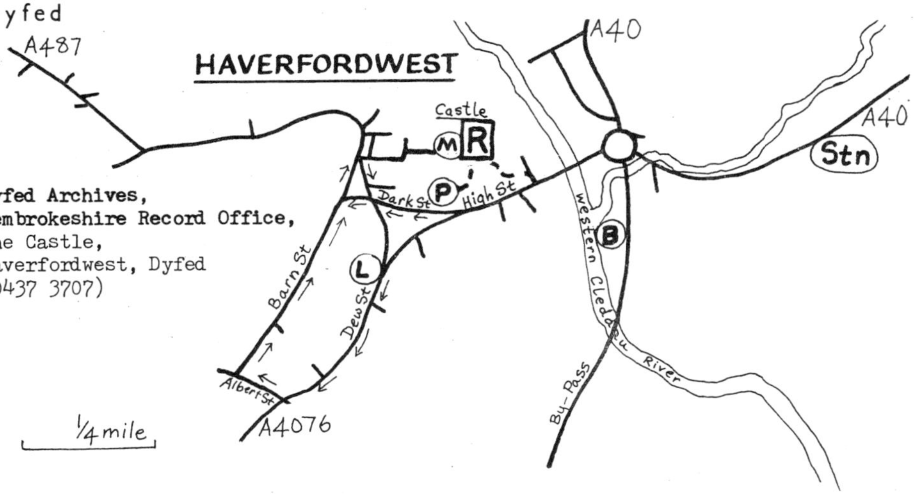

Dyfed Archives,
Pembrokeshire Record Office,
The Castle,
Haverfordwest, Dyfed
(0437 3707)

Glamorgan

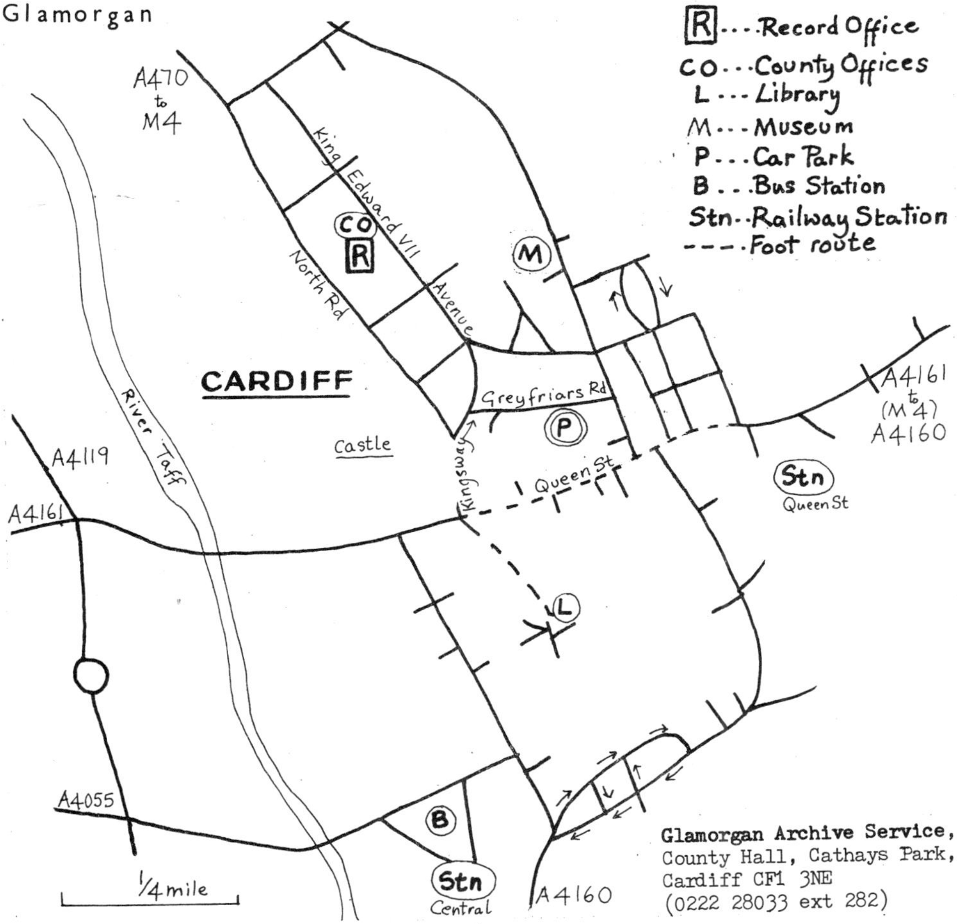

Glamorgan Archive Service,
County Hall, Cathays Park,
Cardiff CF1 3NE
(0222 28033 ext 282)

WALES: Gwent

Gwent County Record Office,
County Hall,
Cwmbran
NP4 2XH
(06333 67711)

Bus service from Newport passes County Hall.

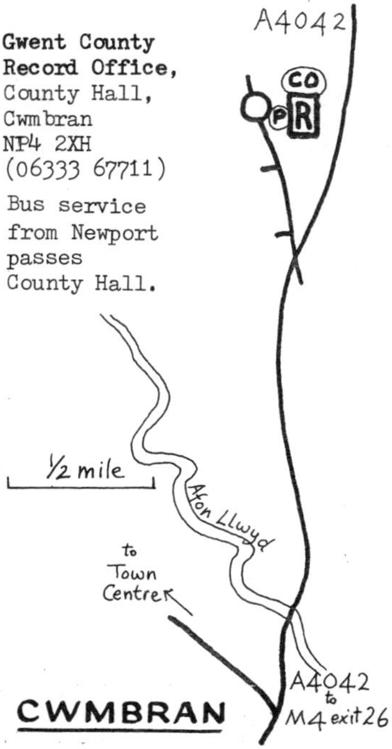

Gwynedd

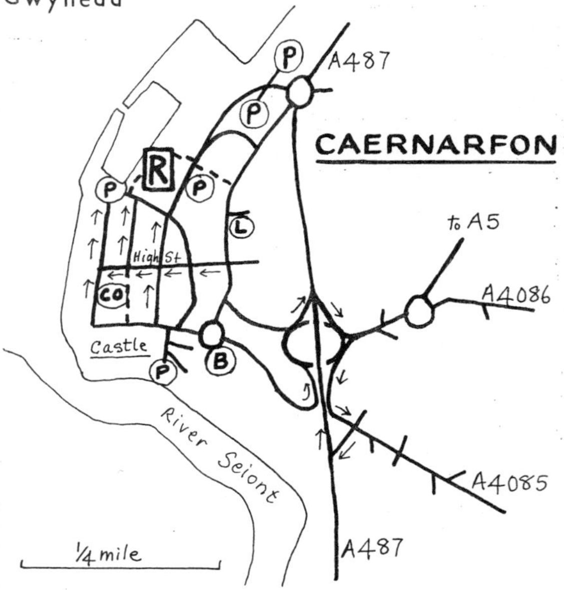

Gwynedd Archives Service,
Caernarfon Area Record Office,
County Offices, Shirehall Street,
Caernarfon LL55 1SH (0286 4121)

R ... Record Office
CO ... County Offices
L ... Library
M ... Museum
P ... Car Park
B ... Bus Station
Stn .. Railway Station
- - - . Foot route

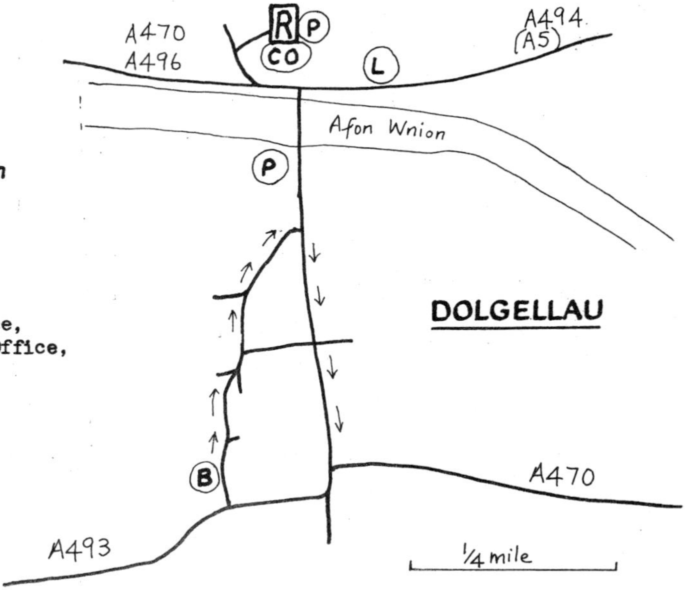

Gwynedd Archives Service,
Dolgellau Area Record Office,
Cae Penarlag,
Dolgellau, Gwynedd
(0341 422341 ext 261)